THE OCCULT TRUTHS OF MYTHS AND LEGENDS

THE OCCULT TRUTHS OF MYTHS AND LEGENDS

GREEK AND GERMANIC MYTHOLOGY
RICHARD WAGNER IN THE LIGHT
OF SPIRITUAL SCIENCE

Sixteen lectures given in Berlin, Cologne and Nuremberg in 1904, 1905 and 1907 (from audience notes)

TRANSLATED AND INTRODUCED BY PAUL KING

RUDOLF STEINER

RUDOLF STEINER PRESS

CW 92

Rudolf Steiner Press
Hillside House, The Square
Forest Row, RH18 5ES

www.rudolfsteinerpress.com

Published by Rudolf Steiner Press 2022

Originally published in German under the title *Die okkulten Wahrheiten alter Mythen und Sagen* (volume 92 in the *Rudolf Steiner Gesamtausgabe* or Collected Works) by Rudolf Steiner Verlag, Dornach. Based on shorthand notes that were not reviewed or revised by the speaker. This authorized translation is based on the first German edition (1999), edited by Helmuth von Wartburg and Ulla Trapp

Published by permission of the Rudolf Steiner Nachlassverwaltung, Dornach

A catalogue record for this book is available from the British Library

ISBN 978 1 85584 604 3

Cover by Morgan Creative
Typeset by Symbiosys Technologies, Vishakapatnam, India
Printed and bound by 4Edge Ltd., Essex

CONTENTS

Editor's Preface

THE lectures in the first part of this volume were given on Fridays to a small circle of members of the Berlin branch, in the apartment of Fräulein Klara Motzkus. The focus of the lectures was Greek and Germanic mythology. From this starting point, however, Rudolf Steiner discusses a great variety of themes, from the unjust death sentence on Socrates to the significance of marriage, and from the founding of Rome to the esoteric background of the work of Wolfram von Eschenbach. What all these discussions had in common was their relation—at times only hinted at, often examined in detail—to the burning questions of the present.

The second part brings together lectures dealing in detail with a specific theme, namely the nature and significance of the music dramas of Richard Wagner. His works, from his earliest attempts to his most mature work *Parsifal*, are examined according to their spiritual content, whereby Steiner stresses that Wagner did not himself have a clear awareness of this deeper meaning, only an indefinite intimation, and that—like the plant growing according to specific laws but unaware of these laws itself—he shaped the Germanic legends with an instinctive, creative and artistic certainty that accords with their deeper, occult meaning.

Introduction

Looking into a myth or legend is like going on a journey of exploration. Each myth has so many levels of depth, and sounding each one takes us more deeply into an aesthetic pleasure, into our psyche, or right into our spiritual history.

Most superficially, we can see myths and legends as 'stories' that can be enjoyed by children, or were told for entertainment around the fire in primitive times now past.

More recently, mythology has been explored in psychology (particularly Jungian psychology) as a means of mining and understanding archetypal patterns in the human psyche. The universal images help shed light on our own sub- and un-conscious, and thus help us harmonize ourselves better into life.

Legends are often a kind of elaborated folk-memory of an actual event (e.g. King Arthur, the Trojan War), the cultural archaeology of a people. But woven into this are strands of deeper meaning, as Steiner points out.

In the lectures in this volume, Steiner goes deeply into the more profound levels of myths and legends. He shows how they can be spiritual depictions of humanity's most ancient evolutionary history, of spiritual forces active at specific evolutionary stages. He shows how they can also be an account of initiation processes. They can even be spiritual wisdom, clothed in pictures in such a way by ancient initiates as to create the capacity in their listeners of being able to understand that same wisdom in a more intellectual form *in a future incarnation*!

It is hard not to be left with a feeling of wonder at the depth and wisdom of the world.

*

Most of Steiner's lectures are available to us as verbatim reports recorded by professional stenographers. The lectures in this volume, however, took place early on in Steiner's lecturing career and consequently in the absence of a stenographer. These printed lectures have therefore been compiled from notes taken by individuals in the audience (see Notes for text sources). Although work was done by the German compilers to keep the text as close as possible to Steiner's actual words, it nevertheless has at times the somewhat aphoristic style of prose compiled from notes. I have tried, nevertheless, to keep close to the German—to its meaning and 'feel'—to reduce as much as possible this second step of separation from the original words.

The lectures were given to members of the Theosophical Society in the time before the establishment of the Anthroposophical Society. Steiner therefore uses terminology that was familiar to his listeners but which he later changed. A case in point is the use of the term 'race'. 'Race' was used in theosophical circles to refer to sequential eras in the development of humanity. In his anthroposophical work Steiner employed different terms to indicate this development in time, rather than a genetic race in the sense we might understand it today.

The changes he made were as follows:

Theosophical term	Steiner's term
1st root race	Polarean age
2nd root race	Hyperborean age
3rd root race	Lemurian age
4th root race	Atlantean age
5th root race	1st Post-Atlantean age
1st sub-race	1. Ancient Indian cultural epoch
2nd sub-race	2. Ancient Persian cultural epoch
3rd sub-race	3. Egypto-Chaldean epoch
4th sub-race	4. Greco-Roman epoch
5th sub-race	5. Fifth Post-Atlantean epoch
6th sub-race	6. Sixth Post-Atlantean epoch
7th sub-race	7. Seventh Post-Atlantean epoch
6th root race	2nd Post-Atlantean age
7th root race	3rd Post-Atlantean age

Paul King

I

Greek And Germanic Mythology

LECTURE 1

BERLIN, 24 JUNE 1904

Good and Evil

I SHOULD like to follow on today from things I discussed a fortnight ago.[1] We might also have the opportunity to talk about the event in Amsterdam.[2] But today I should like to speak about some concrete things we began recently, and which reach into our physical plane.

I have often stressed that the events taking place in our physical world are nothing other than a kind of reflected shadow of what is happening on the higher planes. For the occultist it is clear that he can only understand events in the physical world when he knows what is happening on the supersensory planes. For an occultist who has insight into the higher planes, people appear as though pulled by strings emanating from these higher planes. This might seem to be a restraint on human freedom, but I should like to show today that this is not the case. A few examples can show how the higher worlds influence us.

Here I must refer back to something I said earlier: that, fundamentally speaking, there is no such thing as an absolute good or an absolute evil. Evil is only a kind of 'misplaced' good. When something happened, let's say in the lunar period[3] which preceded our own, and an aspect of that is transplanted into our Earth evolution, it appears in the present time as displaced. It was good during the Moon period but appears evil to us during the Earth phase. During the Moon period someone might have had the task of organizing urges and drives in a harmonious way. But this activity was completed when [Old] Moon came to an end. The task of the Earth period is to master drives and urges from the standpoint of manas [that is, the mental element]. If someone had to live out their urges in the way the pitris[4] had to, in our epoch they would be an evil person, whereas in the lunar epoch they were a wise sage.

People usually don't consider the significance of events like, for example, the appearance of Mohammed, the founder of the Mohammedan religion in the sixth and beginning of the seventh century.

We need to bear in mind here that at first Christianity tried to grow into the various other forms of religion. To begin with we see just a small Jewish community in Palestine; and this remained very small. A principle such as the one contained in Christian teaching is not something folk-souls would easily have imposed upon them. The apostle Paul was able to reach the pagans by initially leaving their thoughts as he found them, and then used their religious forms to imbue them with the Christian essence. In the southern regions of Europe they held services to Mithras; these were similar to the present sacrifice of the Mass. The pagans in those areas adopted Christianity because they could keep their cherished Mithras festival. It was similar with the Germanic peoples and their festival which, as Christmas, became a Christian symbol. Their sanctified ancestors were adopted as Christian saints. In this way Christianity became established in ever-new regions and peoples. It was Christianity's adaptability that made this possible. The Christian religion spread more and more. But because of these many different forms it needed a powerful centre, and this is the Roman papacy. All the harms that were later perpetrated by Christianity are bound up with this world-historical mission of the papacy.

The Semitic peoples had to be reached in a different way, and this is what Mohammed did. He established one initial great precept, saying: 'There are no gods but the One God. The god I teach is the One God.' This precept can only be understood as opposition to Christianity. From the beginning, in its conquering of the physical plane, Christianity had the task of working into the human individuality; it does not build on old forces, but wishes to work through manas.

We see in Mohammedanism that, in a conscious way, there is no longer to be a connection to the ancient, still-spiritual religious forms of paganism, but the right path to conquering the physical plane would now be found only through physical knowledge. We see how this physical knowledge takes hold of medicine, which originates in Arabia and later spreads to other lands. Arabian doctors proceeded from the physical plane, unlike the healers among the Ancient Egyptians, the Druids, and even the Germanic peoples. All these attained to their healing vocation by developing their psychic powers through asceticism and other exercises. We still see something similar today in the practices and procedures of shamanism, but today these have degenerated. So psychic forces were developed in these earlier healers. Mohammed introduced a form of medical practice that derives its remedies purely from the physical plane. This form of medicine was developed where people wanted to know nothing about spiritual beings, only about the One God. Alchemy and astrology as understood in ancient times were done away with and turned into new sciences: into astronomy, mathematics, and so on. These later became the sciences of the Western world. In the Arabs who came to Spain we see people learned about the physical plane, particularly mathematicians. The true adherents of this trend said: 'We honour and reverence what lives in the plant, the animal, and so on, but man should not try clumsily to reproduce what only God is competent to create.' Thus in Moorish art we find only arabesques, figures that don't even have a plant form but are shaped by the imagination.

The power of Greece was superseded by Rome, but Greek education and culture was passed on to the Romans. What the Arabs had, they had received from Mohammed. Mohammed introduced [a form of] science that is permeated purely by the laws of the physical plane. Christian monks received a stimulus from the Moors. Even though the Moors were driven back by political powers, monotheism, which brings with it a deepening of physical science, was brought to Europe by them and led to the purging of all pagan elements from Christianity.

Through Christianity people's feeling-life was led to kama-manas. Through Mohammedanism the intellect, the mind, was led down from the spiritual life to an abstract apprehension of purely physical laws. This physical science had to pass through many stages in order to attain the level it has now. It had to pass through the knowledge of the Vedic priests and through all subsequent stages up to the attainments of our modern time. A lot of it had already been attained by the Atlanteans, albeit by means of psychic forces. This direction towards physical laws has been in preparation ever since Atlantean times.

The Chinese are a residue of the Mongolian race of Atlantis. When we hear the Chinese speak of the TAO, it is something we find hard to understand. The Mongolians of those times had developed a monotheism that went as far as physical tangibility, as feeling the spiritual, and when the Ancient Chinese, the Ancient Mongolian, uttered the word TAO, he felt it as he spoke it. TAO is not 'the Way', as it is usually translated, it is the primary energy (*Grundkraft*) by which the Atlantean could still transform plants, by which he could set his curious airships in motion. This primary energy, which is called *vril*, was used everywhere by the Atlantean, and he called it his God. He felt this energy inside himself, and for him it was 'the Way and the Goal'. Thus every Mongolian regarded himself as an instrument in the hand of the great vril-force.

The monotheism of the Atlanteans was retained by the races that survived the Great Flood. The fifth root-race emerged from this religious form which was still spiritual. But this spiritual religious form that worshipped a unitary god gradually degenerated into polytheism. Monotheism was still to be found only in highly developed priests. At the beginning of Christianity the monks were crafty: Baldur, they said, became man in Palestine. In the early centuries we would have found a Christianity mixed together with all kinds of pagan elements, even in Arian Christianity. This development ensued at the time when a particularly vigorous glow of religious feeling was enkindled in the Ancient Mongolian races by highly developed shamans. As a reaction to polytheism, we see on the one hand the emergence of a new unitary religion in Arabia through Mohammed. On the other hand, somewhat earlier, we see the appearance of an initiated shaman with TAO-consciousness, who makes himself the avenger against those who had lapsed from the old monotheistic idea of God. Attila[5] was called 'the Scourge of God'. We see everywhere in his empire the vassal princes living in pomp and splendour, whereas he, a shaman, lived extremely simply. It was said of him that his eyes blazed and the ground shook when he raised his sword. This great initiate would have been fully justified in Atlantean times; in our times he looks like a criminal. The same energy that at one time is an expression of divine fire, appears in another time as divine wrath. Why do such things happen? They are necessary in order to make any kind of progressive development possible. When an advance is to be made in development, the separate threads—seen from a higher perspective—must harmonize with each other once more.

We have also discussed the Druid priests who instructed their people through stories and myths. They were healers, priests, and astrologers all in one; they had inspired knowledge. As the Celtic element was superseded by Germanic tribes, so the belief in the old form of inspiration also subsided. The men were given the task of conquering the physical plane; they became warriors. We meet intuitive and productive energy in the feminine element. Women became priestesses who were also healers, for example Veleda.[6] All healing at that time was in the hands of women; men were forced out onto the external physical plane. We still find this in the period of the Merovingians and Carolingians. The spiritual element was then suppressed by the science the monks had learnt from the Moors. Between the sixteenth and nineteenth centuries the materialist mode of thought increased more and more. Psychic healers decline; they come into disrepute and are despised as sorcerers and witches. This is connected with a general loss of the ability to heal by psychic means; healing by this path is no longer effective. Paracelsus still had full possession of these abilities.

This is connected with the transition of the guidance of humanity by one Dhyan Chohan [archangel, hierarchical being] of a higher nature to another Dhyan Chohan. Christian esotericism calls this holy Dhyan Chohan 'Saint Michael'; this is the archangel who directs the psychic idealism of humanity. The human being will only be free by realizing that everything that happens on the physical plane is caused by higher forces. He must come into a pupil relationship with the archangel Michael.

Two beings played a role in the Old Testament: the guiding Spirit, which is harmonious, and Beelzebub who is disharmonious although also a Dhyan Chohan—he is the chief of all disharmony on the physical plane; we need to understand him in order to know why one form can work destructively on another. Since the sixteenth century the hosts of Beelzebub have preponderated over the hosts of Michael. Mammon is the god of what hinders people from following the straight path. It would be out of place if this were to continue into the next century.

All physical events are the shadows of supersensory events. The battle between spiritual forces and materialism is a reflection of the battle between the hosts of Beelzebub and Mammon against Michael. This battle had to be fought first on the higher planes. It was won there by Michael thirty years ago, and the present battle here on the physical plane is a reflection of it. Above, the battle has been decided, but for the individual human being it is not finished yet. If the human beings of today are not equal to this, we will all have to perish and new human beings would have to come. This shows us the juncture, the path, that the individual today needs to take.

LECTURE 2

BERLIN, 1 JULY 1904

Reading the Akashic Chronicle
Wolfram von Eschenbach

HAVING said various things of an esoteric nature last Friday by way of preparation, what I have to say today will not seem so strange to you. I would like to discuss an aspect of the history of the last centuries, taken from the Akashic Chronicle. You know that everything that happens is recorded in a certain way in an eternal chronicle in the substance of akasha which is a far more subtle substance than the ones we know. You are aware that all the events of history and prehistory are recorded in this substance. What in theosophical terminology is usually called the *Akashic Chronicle*, is however not the original records, but the reflection of the actual records in astral space. In order to read these, certain requirements are necessary, at least one of which I will talk about.

In order to be able to read the Akashic Chronicle it is necessary to put one's own thoughts at the disposal of the forces and beings which, in theosophical terminology, we call the Masters. It is necessary that the Masters instruct us in how to read the Akashic Chronicle which is written in signs and symbols and not in the words of any existing or former language. As long as we apply the energy we use in ordinary thinking—and every person who has not explicitly learnt to exclude their Ego uses this energy—we will not be able to read the Akashic Chronicle. If you ask yourself 'Who is thinking?', you will have to say, '*I* am thinking.' You connect subject and predicate when you form a sentence. For as long as you connect the separate concepts with each other, you are not in a position to read the

Akashic Chronicle because you are connecting your thoughts with your own Ego. You have to shut off the Ego; you must renounce all sense of your own mode of thinking (*Eigen-Sinn*). You must just take ideas and let the connection between separate ideas arise through forces outside of your self, through the spirit. A renunciation is necessary—not of thinking, but of connecting separate thoughts yourself. Then a Master can come and teach you how to let your thoughts be arranged, by the spirit, into what the universal World-Spirit is able to show of events and things that have taken place in history. When you no longer exercise critical judgement on things, then the universal World-Spirit itself speaks to you, and you place your thought-substance at its disposal.

I now have to talk about something that might arouse prejudices. I must tell you something that is good as a preparation for shutting off the self-willed Ego and thereby learning to read the Akashic Chronicle. You know that something was done by monks in the Middle Ages that is despised today: they sacrificed their intellect. [Medieval] monks did not think in the way modern researchers do. The monks had a specific body of sacred knowledge, holy revealed theology, whose content was given and one did not question it. The theologian of the Middle Ages used his intellect to elucidate and defend the given revelations. No matter how we may regard it today, this was a strict schooling, this sacrificing of the intellect to a given content. We will not go into whether, from a modern point of view, this was something beneficial or objectionable. The monks' sacrifice of the intellect, the exclusion of judgement emanating from the personal 'I', taught them how to put their thoughts at the service of something higher. In a later incarnation what was brought about previously through this sacrifice now comes into effect and gives the person in question the faculty of selfless thought, and makes him a genius at perceiving (*Genie des Anschauens*). If higher vision, Intuition, is added to this, he can use this ability to read the facts in the Akashic Chronicle.

It is most especially interesting to outline once more from this point of view the period in the spiritual development of Europe we discussed eight days ago, namely the period from the ninth to the thirteenth, fourteenth, fifteenth century. If we have attained this selflessness with regard to thought-content, and combined it with the right sense of reverence, of devotion, in the way the mystics were required to do, then the time when great minds appear in world-history often appears very different from [how it is portrayed in] profane history. When we look at this period in the Akashic Chronicle, our gaze is caught by a great figure who can teach us an enormous amount about those times, a figure who is great for the ordinary researcher, but greater still by far for the occultist: Wolfram von Eschenbach.[7]

Wolfram von Eschenbach worked on German, Romance, and Spanish legends. He belonged among the great initiated writers who were selfless enough to work on great existing themes and did not believe they had to create new ones. The great writers like Homer, Sophocles, Euripides, Aeschylus, never had to hunt for themes. Wolfram von Eschenbach belongs among these great writers. In his works he portrays for us the inner spiritual history of the period from the ninth to the fifteenth century. This, externally, is a preparatory period for our modern times in which, as we have seen, everything belonging to the external sense-world is studied. This began with Copernicus. People now began to take the physical plane seriously and not, as hitherto, as a symbol of the higher planes. The worldview of the ancients was not wrong, it was just a view from a different standpoint: they regarded the phenomena of the external world as symbols for devachanic conditions. Copernicus said that we no longer want to see the physical world as a symbol, but want to look at the physical world itself.

Of course, people's whole picture of the world was changed. It was during this time that the focus of attention was prepared that is directed towards what is practical, physical, and material. Earlier cultures, on which our physical life depended for its traditions and authorities, made a transition into a culture where the important thing was personal aptitude. Previously, a farmer's son had standing because he was a farmer's son; a knight's son inherited the privileges of his ancestors. This changed during this period. This is the period of the founding of towns. Everywhere people streamed together and founded towns; the middle class expanded, practical inventions appear—the pocket-watch, the printing press.

But this is only the external aspect. People's souls were directed towards the practicality of knowledge, as seen in Copernicus, and which developed further in the Enlightenment, and politically in the French Revolution. The merchant classes pursued practical interests for which a personal aptitude was necessary. What one's father did was no longer so important. For one who investigates things in the Akashic Chronicle, it is clear that what occurs on the physical plane is directed from the higher planes. The leading minds are influenced by initiates who work on the higher planes. Behind individuals of genius we find high beings who work behind the scenes from the White Lodge. The physical aspect is only the external side. The inner side is the work of the highest initiates of the White Lodge and their emissaries who go forth into the world.

I should like briefly to describe this occult hierarchy. We have there beings that are never seen: the Masters. For people on the physical plane, they cannot be perceived. Among these [people on the physical plane] are chelas, occult pupils, who undertake to carry out onto the physical plane the great commissions of the Masters. The first who teach there are called *hamsas*,[8] which means *swans*. The chelas who are called *homeless*, are so called because their home is not in this world but on the higher planes. They give people the teachings they themselves have received from the hamsas. They are the emissaries for the geniuses in world history. Thus, for example, it can be verified that there was a connection between the leaders of the French Revolution and this spiritual side of history.

The great White Lodge had to send out its emissaries to prepare and give teaching to the people, so that they could become the organs on the physical plane for carrying out the will of the Masters. This was also the case with Wolfram von Eschenbach. The existence of the White Lodge was known about in the Middle Ages, and at that time was called the *Grail Castle*. In it was the White Brotherhood. The one who was sent out at that time to carry out the founding of towns on the physical plane was called Lohengrin. He was taught directly by a hamsa, and gave teaching [in turn] to Henry I [9] who was known as a founder of towns. This meant that the souls of the time were to receive a new characteristic from the 'homeless one'.

In the language of occultism the soul is always symbolized by a female figure. Elsa von Brabant represents the soul of those times. She was to be married to a knight, Telramund, who belonged to the old tradition. But an emissary of the Grail comes and frees Elsa von Brabant, the soul of the times. Through Wolfram von Eschenbach['s work] this time is characterized by Henry being led to Rome where inward, esoteric Christianity is fighting the great enemy of Christianity, the Saracens. Lohengrin is a 'homeless one' whom one is not allowed to ask whence he comes. It goes against the obligations of his Order to ask him. He has a kind of Janus head: on the one hand he must look to the occult Brotherhood, and on the other hand to the people he has to guide in the physical world. Richard Wagner often found poignant words as when, for example, Lohengrin sings, 'Receive my thanks, my dear swan.' This is the moment when the swan leaves him, and he becomes dependant on physical conditions. He is placed in a world that is not quite appropriate for him; it is not his true world. His world is the world of the other side, so he must be regarded as homeless. When his mission is fulfilled, the homeless one returns whence he came. When his origin is revealed, he must leave. This is hard for one who has entered into relationship with the physical plane. Hence Elsa von Brabant has to ask him three times where he comes from.

Thus we see that this period is depicted by the initiate Wolfram von Eschenbach in its association with the higher planes. Lohengrin is the emissary, the messenger of the Grail knights. The Grail knights are the White Lodge on Montsalvat. It was the task of the emissaries of the Grail, the Grail knights, to renew again and again the ancient traditions of genuine, true Christianity. This is what was borne in mind when the Grail Castle and the Holy Grail were spoken about. The Grail knights were imagined as the defenders of what had come into the world through a proper Christianity. This is indicated in the Gospel of John: 'the Word became flesh.'[10] What was transfigured and glorified by Christ was physical existence itself; he came into the physical world. The other great individuals were teachers of humanity: Buddha, Zarathustra, Pythagoras, Moses—they were all teachers. They are 'the Way and the Truth'; but only Christ in an occult sense is 'the Life'. Hence he says, 'No-one cometh unto the Father save by me.'[11] A healing of Life could only take place when the Word entered directly into the human body. This bringing-down of the divine onto the physical plane was to be renewed again and again by the White Lodge. Thus the Grail chalice is portrayed as the same chalice from which Jesus served the Last Supper, and in which Joseph of Arimathea collected the blood [of Christ] on Golgotha. In this way the principle of Christianity was to be preserved and to live on, and was to receive new energy through twelve Grail knights who, following on from the apostles, were sent forth as emissaries to undertake new tasks.

The way of seeing things throughout the Middle Ages was that when an important stage of civilization was to be reached, a chela, a 'swan', would have to impart teaching to the people. This is how Wolfram von Eschenbach saw and portrayed history. Anyone who is able to read between the lines of Wagner's *Lohengrin*, will find that Wagner felt intuitively—not intellectually but feelingly—that there was something great here. This is why he believed in a renewal of art by associating it with what is superhuman. In the Middle Ages this was depicted by showing that when Elsa von Brabant tried to hold Lohengrin in this world, he withdrew and, according to Eschenbach, went to India. In the end, the Grail Castle too was imagined to be in India. It is also said of the Rosicrucians that, when they withdrew at the end of the eighteenth century, they had gone to Asia, to the Orient. This is the history of the founding of towns in the Middle Ages according to the record in the Akashic Chronicle. Details might be described differently by others, but in broad outline they will always agree.

Lecture 3

BERLIN, 8 JULY 1904

Sacramentalism
Daedalus and Icarus

Is the knowledge taught by theosophy something that has particular importance and relevance for a larger circle of people in general, or is theosophy something that can only be for a few interested individuals? This question leads us to a theme very seldom discussed but which needs to be discussed: namely, so-called sacramentalism and the particular task of our present root-race. The question is: What is sacramentalism, and how is our purely human task related to it? We could ask what it means to some craftsman who works all day in a cabinetmaker's workshop to know that Lohengrin, as the emissary of the Holy Grail, once inspired the most important cultural movements of the Middle Ages. What significance does all this talk about high spiritual goals have for the broad mass of people? The question is answered when we understand the nature of sacramentalism.

Following on from the outlook of the Greeks, I should like to speak today about the emergence of our present post-Atlantean root-race in relation to the preceding Atlantean root-race, and add something concerning the significance of sacramentalism. You all know the legend of Daedalus and Icarus, and the legend of Theseus. I should like to touch on the immensely profound meaning behind the legend of Daedalus and Icarus.

The legend relates how there was once a man called Daedalus who was able to create works of art that were alive, statues that could see and hear, machines that moved by themselves. Daedalus was able to do all this. He was esteemed throughout the land, but he was also exceptionally ambitious. He had a nephew, Talus, whom he trained, but who quickly surpassed him in certain ways. We are told that Talus was able to use a potter's wheel, and also had certain skills that were alien to Daedalus. For example, Talus looked carefully at the lower jaw of a snake and got the idea to use the snake's teeth to make a saw. Thus he became the inventor of the saw. When we compare the character of Daedalus with that of Talus we see things in Daedalus that have become alien to our fifth root-race. Talus, by contrast, invents things that belong to the technical skills of the fifth root-race. If we make a comparison with the fourth root-race, the Atlanteans, we see how the Atlanteans had the ability to employ the vril-force in the way that we use steam to drive locomotives, machines, and so on. The post-Atlantean era has lost this ability. Our time, on the other hand, has the modern ability to assemble inorganic objects into machines. It is this transition that the legend is telling us about. Daedalus then manages to make wings of a kind, with which he can lift himself above the Earth. His son Icarus also wants to do this, but he does not succeed; he is destroyed by it. This comparison, for the Greek mind, shows that different ages of our earthly development have different tasks. If a particular era of earthly evolution tried to adopt a task appropriate to another time, it would be destroyed by it. Everything in its place, everything in its time.

Now, the Greek Daedalus legend is associated with something else. After he has killed Talus, Daedalus goes to Minos on Crete. There is a monster there, the Minotaur. The Minotaur stands in contrast to the Sphinx. The Minotaur has a bull's head and a human body; the Sphinx has a human head and an animal's body. The Minotaur has to be held in check from the devastation it wreaks. Daedalus has to contain it. He does this by building a labyrinth. The Minotaur has to be fed human flesh. Every nine years, seven youths and seven maidens have to be sacrificed to it.

The Minotaur legend is associated with the legend of Theseus. Theseus was the son of Aegeus. Aegeus had told Theseus to retrieve the sword and sandals which Aegeus had hidden under a great rock. After doing many deeds in Athens, Theseus goes to Crete in order to conquer the Minotaur and free the city of Athens from its obligation to provide the seven youths and seven maidens. The Greeks always looked to Crete for something very particular. It was from Crete that Lycurgus[12] learnt the laws, which he brought back to Sparta, for a kind of communistic commonwealth, for Crete was thought to have a constitution that was typical of all the ancient hierocractic states that renounced all personal possession. The original foundation of every religion is associated with a kind of communism. Even Plato still looked to Crete as the seat of a model constitution.[13] This hierocratic constitution is a remnant of ancient Atlantean institutions. Daedalus was able to restrain what was causing devastation in Crete because he was acquainted with Atlantean life. We must see in the Minotaur a representation of black magic in Crete. This was now to cease. The Athenians no longer wished to send seven youths and seven maidens to Crete. Theseus' ship set out with black sails. Once he had conquered the Minotaur he wanted to hoist a white sail instead of the previous black one. Black magic was to become white. Theseus manages the undertaking with the help of Ariadne's thread, and returns to Athens [but he forgets to use the white sail]. The Greeks were not yet so advanced as to be fully worthy of the white path. Love is supposed to reign in Ariadne's thread. But already at that time an indication towards Christianity is made in such a way that the Love Principle—Ariadne—is stolen by Bacchus who has not yet developed the principle that was to be spread by Christianity. Theseus, like Hercules, was a Hero, a Sun-runner (*Sonnenläufer*), an initiate of the sixth grade.[14]

In Greece a complex of legends of this nature was the property of the common people. The general populace knew these legends. Why did the priests seek to incorporate cosmic secrets into legends? Every priest would have felt it to be unholy, indeed impossibly profane, to put anything into a story that did not have deep meaning. The priests were aware that the deep meaning could not be immediately apparent to the common folk. The people were told fables, fairy tales, myths—there was deep meaning in these. A fundamental hallmark of the tales of the ancients is that the farther back we go, the deeper the meaning becomes. There was no such thing in those times as a tale without deep meaning. It was only later times that departed from this priestly view and produced works no longer containing anything of these spiritual secrets. Even things presented in the market place were to be those that flowed from the spiritual life. When we bear this in mind, we can say that in those times there was as yet no leadership other than that given by priests. Only later was the priest-king superseded by a secular king. This brought with it the transition from the ancient priest-king state to a state ruled by a secular king—*archon*[15] means king-ruler.

The legend of the founding of Rome exemplifies this way of seeing things. The way people thought about history in antiquity was not one where one related external events. Only after Herodotus[16] was history related as a chronicle. Previously this did not happen. Everything was presented symbolically. At that time what eyes saw and ears heard was to be regarded as something higher, as the expression of the spiritual. When a priest tried to elucidate the origins of the Romans, he related the following: Always, when something like this is to realize itself, the seven holy principles of the cosmos come into effect. Everything happens in a succession of the seven principles. At the beginning, the divine founder descends from heaven. Then priests extract what is a living element in the matter; this then lives as kama [earthly desire]. Then manas, reason, is born in the kama. The body, which is itself a holy thing, lives in heaven. It only becomes unholy when it is misused. These are the four lower principles. Then the three higher ones have to enter. Something that is more perfect, more complete, must descend.

This is also what happened with the founding of Rome.[17] First came Romulus; he came from heavenly spheres and was the founder. Rome was an off-shoot of Ancient Troy. King Numitor of Alba Longa was a descendent of Aeneas who had fled from Troy and landed in Latium. We just need to understand the words: *alba longa* is the long white garment of Catholic priests. *Amulius* means 'the unwed one', the priest. So Rome was a hierocratic daughter-city of Troy. Numitor is the will element in the human being. He was first exiled to the forest but then became the ancestor of the founders of Rome. Romulus is the founder of Roman culture, the first king.

He was numbered among the gods under the name of Quirinus. The second king was Numa Pompilius. The third king was Tullus Hostilius; he is the representative of kama; at that time war was predominant; there developed what in theosophy is called kama-rupa. The fourth king was Ancus Martius—he is the representative of kama-manas. Technological things were made. When the fourth principle was sufficiently mature, Etruscan culture was introduced. Tarquinius Priscus, the fifth king, brings manas. Under him the great buildings and the water supply were constructed. What is called manas is represented in Tarquinius Priscus. The sixth principle is buddhi. This brings about the blessings of human co-existence through love and what is just. Servius Tullius was the sixth king of the Romans. He was the one who created order and laid down laws along the lines of the Etruscans. The seventh king was Tarquinius Superbus, 'the Proud', who was overthrown.

This is how the priests viewed the arising of Rome. It was not an interpretation but a reality. The governance of the cities was such that the seven principles were what guided the rulers. If something is to thrive on Earth, it must be created in sequence of the seven principles. A priest would never have done anything that was for his successor to do. This was all written in the temple books which were called the Sibylline Books.[18] This was the plan, as it were, of history. The priests had to follow the Sibylline Books.

We see here the realization of spiritual forces which lived in this priest culture. We see that the world is directed and guided by spirit. It was only later that people lost their understanding of spiritual regency. It is said of Tages,[19] the principal Etruscan god, that he rose out of the ground of a freshly ploughed field. Technical construction and applied arts were the hallmark of Etruscan culture. Every stone of Etruscan architecture shows there is something special here. They aimed at bearing the greatest weight with the least amount of material. This is the principle behind Etruscan architecture, its domes and arches. This culture, which was spiritually guided, descended to the physical plane. Individual aptitude now came to the forefront. All awareness of the connection between the most mundane act and the spiritual, ceased. It is clear to an occultist whether or not a person in a particular job has heard something of divine intention and purpose, and whether they have absorbed some of what has flowed out of the spiritual, because such a person performs the most everyday task differently from someone in whom this is not the case. The consecration that pours down from the higher spheres onto earthly life does not pour out in the same way for those who adhere only to the physical plane.

The essence of sacramentalism is that the human being fills everyday things with a sacred spiritual quality. The sense and point of the ancient legends was to bring about the right vibration in people's souls, so that they were filled with spiritual strength. Through this, the simplest action of a naive heart can be hallowed. This has effects and will always continue to do so. One who knows this also knows that our culture needs to turn around. We can try as hard as we like to bring harmony and order to the physical plane, but it will fail as long as we work only on the physical plane; harmony created on the one side gives rise to disharmony on the other. But if you let the spiritual operate, you will see that everyday matters are approached in a completely different way. This is sacramentalism.

This idea is also behind Christian sacramentalism: healing from the spiritual plane. A sacrament is a physical act that is carried out in such a way that a spiritual process is symbolically expressed in it. It is a symbolism that has its justification on higher planes. There is nothing arbitrary in a sacrament. Even in its smallest details it is a reflection of a higher occult procedure. Anyone who wishes to understand a sacrament in which the ceremonial aspect is a reflection of a spiritual event, must acquaint themself with what lies behind it. It is an occult procedure that eludes our external eyes. In all sacramentalism there is not only something rational or intellectual taking place, but something that has a real occult significance.

Let us take for example the occult significance of fire. In the earliest periods of evolution there was no fire. Fire only emerged when the Earth had condensed to the point where earthly matter existed that could catch fire. Hence the discovery of fire is portrayed as a process of our fifth root-race.

Prometheus brought fire down from heaven. Making fire has given our culture its character. Just imagine how things would be if we had no fire. Everything of a rational and technological nature in our development is thanks to fire. Fire is that which brings things down to the physical plane. Material culture is due to fire.

And so the priests had to see something special in fire. For this reason, in the second post-Atlantean cultural epoch, the Persian magi saw that fire, above all, contained an element that was needed in the sacraments. What did the Persian priest bring about through ceremonial procedures at the altar? Occultism knows that there were seven Zoroasters. The Zoroaster known to history is the seventh. The Persian magus had a special way of generating fire. This procedure was a reflection of the great cosmic emergence of fire. There stood the Persian magus with his thyrsus and performed his ceremonies which every occultist knows well—but only occultists. This procedure was a reflection of the great cosmic emergence of fire. When, in the priest training schools, they no longer understood how to generate fire with the thyrsus, they looked for fire from a source in nature. Initially they got fire from lightning, and then propagated it through the so-called eternal flame where [new flame] was only allowed to be lit from [the old]. Fire obtained from nature was thought to be more effective than fire produced artificially. During an epidemic in animals in England in 1826, and in Hanover in 1828, people made fire by rubbing wood because they believed that the [healing] herbs they boiled on it would be more efficacious.

People need to create a spiritual life again that reaches into every hand movement and every step; and introducing this once more is the task and aspiration of the spiritual movement. The sacramental attitude of earlier times must return. We need to realize that there is a difference in acting out of the spirit or out of matter. Letting spiritual life flow once more—that is our goal.

Lecture 4

BERLIN, 15 JULY 1904

Germanic Mythology

IF we go back in the evolution of the [human] race, you know that we come to the root-race of Atlantis whose empire now lies at the bottom of the Atlantic Ocean. And if we go even further back, we come to the Lemurian root-race. This is a race that you must think of as being completely different in its organization from our present root-race, and even from the Atlanteans. The Lemurians lived on a continent that extended southwards from the Indian subcontinent and South-East Asia, and is today also the floor of an ocean. A few descendants of this population are still to be found in Australia.

But where must we look for the second root-race? Here we need to bear in mind that the third race, the Lemurians, already looked completely different from us, and also completely different from the Atlanteans, the fourth race. The Lemurians did not have what we would call memory, ideas, intellect; they only had this in a seminal condition. The second race, on the other hand, was gifted with a high spirituality, which was, however, not located in their heads, but can be pictured like a constant revelation from outside. The people of this second race were called the Hyperboreans. They inhabited the area around the North Pole—in Siberia, Northern Europe, including the area that is now sea. And if you imagine this land with a kind of tropical temperature, you get a rough idea of what it was like at that time. It was originally populated by people who as individuals wandered about like beings in a dream. If they had been left to themselves, they would have been able to do nothing. There was wisdom, as it were, in the air, in the atmosphere.

Only in the Lemurian age did a marriage take place between wisdom and the soul element; so before this we need to picture all mental or spiritual awareness in humankind as fog-like. Here were the seeds of the misty mind, and the seeds of the light-mind. The spirituality that emerged as seed in the sons of the fire-mist, which still appears familiar to us, must be sought in the southern regions in Lemuria. In the regions north of us there lived peoples that had a dream-consciousness that was clearer than Pitri-consciousness.[20] In general we must not imagine that the peoples living up there [in the North] stayed there. They undertook migrations southwards. And these migrations still continued long into the times in which the Lemurian race emerged in the south. There was a northern Lemurian race, so to speak, and a southern Lemurian race. There were twelve migrations. These great migrations gradually brought the inhabitants of the different regions into contact. They also brought people into regions not far from our own, into regions we would call Central Germany, France, Central Russia, and so on.

You need to be clear that we are talking here about a time when what we call the higher animals already existed. The Lemurians were described as a kind of giant, and they came into contact with the people coming from the north. Two races arose from this. There arose a race which, in humanity's prehistory, became the foundation of the Atlanteans. All these peoples mixed at that time in present-day Europe. We must not imagine this to be as simple as it seems when put into words. Now, from this mixture of Hyperboreans, Lemurians, and later also of Atlanteans, there emerged initiates who were different from the initiates we look on as our teachers today; these latter stem essentially from the south, from the Lemurian continent.

In the North there developed what I would call a kind of mist world, and the three chief initiates that we must look for on this island of humanity, were called, even still in the time when Christianity was first emerging: Odin, Vili, and Ve. These are the three great Nordic initiates. They traced their origin in a very regular way—like the general populace, we could say—to the earthly realm in which everything was contained in an unmixed state that is now distributed among all people. One could say that, in a way similar to the general populace, a race arose in this realm of the earth that was very dissimilar to present-day humanity. This race was governed by an All-Wisdom. The teacher-priests called this All-Wisdom the *All-Father*. Two realms were spoken of: Niflheim and Muspelheim. Niflheim is the misty region of the North, the dawning mist-filled conditions of the Hyperborean root-race, in contrast to Muspelheim. Legend tells of twelve rivers, which dammed themselves up and then turned to ice. From this arose a human race represented by the giant Ymir, and also an animal species, the cow Audumbla. From Ymir arose the sons of the frost giants. Human beings who were endowed with reason emerged later—this accords also with *The Secret Doctrine*.[21] And so the Germanic legend also relates that [the offspring of Ymir and Audumbla], Odin, Vili, and Ve, walked by the sea and created man. This is referring to the human beings of *The Secret Doctrine* who only arose later and who were endowed with reason.

There is an ancient truth in this primordial Germanic legend. We are also told how later there were two great migrations from the Far East to the West [and from the West to the East]. We have to imagine that first of all there was a Celtic population which then established colonies. These original Celts were fully under the influence of their initiates. The initiates spread the original teachings about Odin, Vili, and Ve and their priesthoods. The Celts had priests we call Druids. The Druids were centred in a great Lodge, in the North Lodge. This is preserved in the legend of King Arthur and the Round Table. This Lodge of the northern initiates really existed, the holy Lodge of Ceridwen[22]—the White Lodge of the North. Later it was called the Order of Bards. This Lodge continued to exist into much later times, and was only dissolved during the reign of Elizabeth I. Then the Order withdrew from the physical plane entirely. This was the source of all the Germanic sagas. All Germanic poetry can be traced to the original Lodge of Ceridwen, which was also called the Magic Cauldron of Ceridwen. An individual who had the greatest influence right into the first centuries after the birth of Christ, was the great initiate Meredin, who is preserved for us in the name of the magician Merlin.[23] He was called 'the magician of the Northern Lodge'.

This is all contained in ancient Celtic mystery teachings; there you find an indication of what the initiates of the East had to give. And what was given back to them by the Celts was the Baldur myth, the myth of the god of light and the god of darkness. In this way the initiates of the West gradually introduced these myths to the initiates of the East, with the well-considered intention of telling them something of significance. And in the belief that something must follow this, they added to this myth something that lay in the future, namely the fall of the gods. Baldur could not withstand this fall. So a second migration was prepared for after the Twilight of the Gods. It was said that a new Baldur would arise, and this 'new Baldur' foretold to the people is none other than Christ. These things could not develop at the same time in the North as they did in the South, in Greece for example. In the North it was more the masculine gods that were revered, and in the South more the cultus of beauty. The whole Northern element had a particular quality that had long been present but which at the same time was the seed of its undoing: its warlike nature. So in the North we have Odin, Vili, and Ve, and alongside them is Loki. Loki is the desire element, wish, and this gives the Northern world a warlike nature which has the element of the Valkyries within it. They ignite enthusiasm for battle. They are something the Northern element always had. Loki was the son of desire; Hagen is a later form of the original Loki.

And now a few words on the nature of initiates in those times. When someone was initiated, thereby becoming acquainted with spiritual powers, people expressed this by saying, 'He has undertaken the journey into the realm of the good dead, into the elven realm, to Alfgard, so as to fetch the gold of Niflheim'—gold is the symbol of wisdom. Siegfried was the initiate of the old Germanic element at the time when Christianity was spreading. He was actually invulnerable, but had one spot where he could be wounded, because in this Nordic initiation Loki was still present, the god of desires, in the form of Hagen. Hagen is the one who kills the initiate on his weak spot. In the Nibelung Saga, Brunhilde is a similar figure, a female goddess similar to Pallas Athene in Greece. In the North she signifies the embodiment of the wild, slaying element of battle.

In Siegfried you have the old Germanic initiate. The element of combat is expressed in old Germanic knighthood. Because it was predominantly a worldly element, worldly knighthood—even into the eight, ninth, tenth, eleventh century—had to trace its origins to Siegfried the initiate. The origin of this class of knights was the Round Table of King Arthur. This is where the great knights came from—or rather, those that wanted to become leading knights in the world had to go to King Arthur's Round Table. There they learnt worldly wisdom; but eagerness for combat, the Loki-Hagen element, was mixed in with it.

Something was to be particularly prepared in the Germanic element, which was able to come to expression most especially in the Nordic element. It was possible to prepare something here that was connected with the development of human beings on the physical plane. We know that what took place there was the descent of the highest principle to the physical plane; the form taken by this highest principle, on the physical plane, is the personal element. Thus the personal element developed, personal prowess in combat, which was perhaps most highly developed in Hagen.

Let's go back to the Lemurians. The Lemurians did not yet have what people today call love. Love between a man and a woman did not exist. There was certainly sexuality, but love was only later to sanctify sexuality. Love in its present meaning did also not yet exist among the Atlanteans. Only when the personal element had gained such importance could love develop. Towards the end of the Lemurian period, in certain regions, they had a curious system. The people living in a particular region were systematically divided into four groups. These groups were so construed that an individual in the first group—let's call it group A—was never allowed to marry anyone from group B. Individuals in group A had to marry someone from group C, and people in group B someone from group D. Personal inclination was thereby avoided; the personal element was excluded. This division was instituted in the service of all humanity. At that time it contained nothing of personal love. Only slowly did personal wishes develop in love; and this was the love that descended fully to the physical plane, and was prepared for at that time.

The farther back in time you go, the more you will find that eroticism plays a minor role. Even in the early period of Greek poetry it plays almost no role at all. But it played a particular role in German poetry of the Middle Ages. You see love portrayed there in two forms: you see it portrayed as courtly love (*Minne*) and as desire. The blows of fate that Siegfried had to suffer were the result of the emergence of the personal element. Go back to Rome and you will find that the grounds for marriage were completely different. In Greece too, personal love was unknown to begin with; it only emerged later.

Then Christianity came to Central Europe. We saw that in Central Europe Christianity was introduced while still preserving what was there before. The idea of the figure of Baldur slowly changed into the idea of the figure of Christ. This happened over a number of generations. Boniface thus found a ground already prepared.[24]

The legend of King Arthur and his Round Table gradually became associated with the legend of the Holy Grail. This association was brought about by an actual initiate of the thirteenth century—by Wolfram von Eschenbach.[25] The Siegfried initiation was still the old initiation. Worldly knighthood still played a role here, as did the danger of being betrayed by the element of desire and narcissism. Only once one had overcome this element, once one had done away with it entirely, and had ascended from the principle of worldly knighthood to the principle of spiritual knighthood, could one attain to spiritual initiation. Eschenbach portrays this in Parzival. To begin with, Parzival is part of worldly knighthood. His father is killed by treachery on a Crusade to the East. Behind this is the fact that his father was indeed seeking for higher initiation; but because he still had in himself the element of the old initiation, he was betrayed. Parzival's mother, Herzeleide, tried to keep him away from the physical plane; she puts a fool's cap on his head. Parzival is nevertheless caught up in the stream of worldly knighthood and comes to the court of King Arthur. That Parzival is destined for the Christian stream is indicated by the fact that he comes to the castle of the Holy Grail. He has been given an important lesson: not to ask too many questions. This signifies nothing other than finding the point of inner stillness, of having inner tranquillity and peace, and to stop going around the outer world full of curiosity. So Parzival doesn't ask any questions because he wishes to gain access to the castle. And so, initially, he is rejected. But then he does eventually come to the ailing Amfortas. He is taken higher by Christian initiation.

No matter where you open Wolfram von Eschenbach's book, you find everywhere that he was an initiate. He joined together these two legend cycles because he knew that what we call the union of the Arthur Lodge with the Grail Lodge had already taken place. The Arthur Lodge has merged completely into the Grail Lodge.

LECTURE 5

BERLIN, 22 JULY1904

Reincarnation

TODAY I should like to talk about something that is distantly connected with what we have spoken about before. Even though the theosophical movement has already existed for 29 years,[26] it is still the case that its basic teachings are often misunderstood. The teachings on reincarnation, for example, are often understood by those who perhaps have never heard anything more than the name or a few notions, as though we were teaching the transmigration of souls through all kinds of different bodies, including animal bodies. This becomes an accusation, as it were, against us.

Reincarnation into animal bodies was taught in Egypt and in Greece, and we cannot ignore the fact that it can still be found in India as an external teaching. It is true and cannot be disputed that everywhere in esoteric teachings it is said that what we call the human soul has passed through stages of evolution which are supposed to have occurred in animal bodies. This seems to be particularly supported by the highly interesting fact that the origin of the vast majority of all folk-tales, sagas and fables can be traced back to India. If you look at the animal fables and other folk- and fairy tales of very different European countries, you will of course find greater or lesser variations; but you will see that the foundation of many European folk-tales is to be found in the books of Ancient India. This is no great surprise for us since the cultures that the fifth root-race has in common have come to Europe via the Gobi Desert, Egypt and Greece. It is also no surprise for us that the initiates of different nations presented their teachings in the form of fables. But we must be clear what meaning fables have that are set in the animal world. This shines a new light for you on the problem of reincarnation, which may not be generally known.

Indian culture spread over the whole world, even if today it is felt to be something foreign. You can see this in the fact that Buddha was included early on among the Catholic saints under the name of Josaphat. This happened many centuries ago. Due to John of Damascus,[27] who described Buddha's life in his legends of the saints, Buddha's teachings were absorbed into Catholic Christianity. Only the external expression of Buddhism was rejected. This can show us what an enormous significance Indian culture has had for the whole fifth root-race.

There is a large collection of many hundreds of fables—the Jataka tales.[28] In these fables, in the form in which they were spread in past centuries throughout India, Buddha always plays a role. We are told that Buddha was incarnated as this or that animal, how he lived here or there as one animal or another, what his actions were in this animal world, and how he remembered it. Then there is usually a moral lesson about how one should act in a similar situation. The fable form was considered an exemplary educational tool for the sons of kings. These pedagogical methods were also used in Europe.

You all know the tale that when we look at the moon we can see an animal shape there. At any rate, many people see an animal shape there. The most common one is the hare. How the hare came to be in the moon is told in various ways. This also has its origin in the Indian Jataka tales. [The story goes that] in one of his many previous lives, Buddha was once a hare. He lived in a forest with three friends. His first friend was a jackal, his second friend, an ape, and his third friend, an otter. So he lived with these three friends, and even as a hare he was already a very advanced being so he was able to educate the other animals in many various ways. He gave them teaching, and taught above all that one should observe the holy feast days and make an offering on them. He said to them:

> 'Above all you must see that you save some of your food and give it to those who come to you begging, so that on holy feast days you can make your offering in a worthy manner.'

> Now, a feast day was approaching. One of the animals went into a neighbouring region and saw people busy gathering fish for food. When the people had gone away, the animal thought to itself, 'Surely I can take some. But I will make sure,' thought the animal, and said, 'Does this food belong to anyone?' Since nobody answered, it took some of the food.
>
> The second animal did likewise, and so did the third.
>
> Now the foretold feast days arrived. The god Indra disguised himself as a Brahmin and went to visit the animals.
>
> Indra came to the first animal and asked, 'Can you give me some food for the offering?' The animal related how it had found the food. Then Indra said, 'I will come back later and take some of the food.'
>
> In the same way, he went to the second and the third animal.
>
> But the hare had only eaten some grass, and said to itself, 'If someone comes to ask me for something, I can't give them grass. I will offer myself as food.'
>
> Now, when Indra came to him and asked him for something, the hare said, 'I have nothing I can give you, but I offer you myself as food. Make a fire, and you will be able to roast me and then dine on me. All I ask is that you see that no harm comes to any insects which might be on me.'
>
> Indra saw from this how morally advanced the hare was and brought it about that the fire could not harm him, so that the hare remained completely unscathed. As the hare thus had the god Indra before him, he said, 'O wise god Indra, remain here, and together we will proclaim the teachings.'
>
> And the god Indra answered, 'Yes, we will proclaim them in such a way that it will be impossible to extinguish them during this whole cosmic age.' And he took a pen and drew a hare in the moon that is visible now for the whole cosmic age.

So that is the fable of Buddha, who is transposed into the animal world as a hare, and who sacrificed himself completely. A fable of this nature would engrave itself deeply in the minds of those who heard it told, in order to prepare them for a later incarnation; souls became mature enough to then seek the truth themselves. This was the whole point of fables. Originally, fables were not told in the way they are told today, where we have no notion why the animal behaves as it does. Far rather, the stories were told so that, in the telling, people experienced certain images in their minds which have an effect on the causal body, and emerge in a following life as a sense for truth. Fables were not told to give people an aesthetic pleasure but to prepare their souls so that when they were reborn after many years, they could absorb the truth more easily. For such a fable to have this kind of meaning, for it to create the spiritual form, as it were, so that later pure truth could be absorbed, it had itself to contain pure truth, otherwise the vibrations that enable people later to absorb the real truth would not be stimulated in their astral body and causal body. There is such an uncommonly profound meaning in precisely this fable, and it is composed with such poetic subtlety, that we would have to wonder greatly at the Ancient rishis if we did not know that they were men taught by devas. And we should also have to wonder at it if we did not know that these fables are connected with a basic fact: namely, the relationship of the human soul to all other beings of nature.

Consider how the whole process of our earthly life has taken its course. We are now in the fourth round;[29] this was preceded by the third, second, and first rounds. We human beings already existed in the first round but not in the form of our existence today. We had a substantially different form. We came over as pitris from a previous planet and began our earthly course in the first round. That's where we passed through the mineral kingdom. As pitris we were able to collaborate in the work on the mineral kingdom which was created at that time. The mineral kingdom looked very different then from how it does today. There were no crystal forms; all physical substances were in a mineral-elemental condition, including those from which human, animal and plant-bodies arose. In this first round there were no living plants as yet, no animals, no human beings—with regard to their outer form,—everything was alive there in soul, but not yet in form. The forms that were created in the first round, and which later became our skeletal system, were prepared by the pitris as a mineral substructure.

In the second round, the pitris prepared their plant substructure. Everything that was later modelled into our digestive and respiratory systems did not have the form it has today, but was prepared as a substructure. Alongside this, the mineral kingdom continued to shape itself as a kind of independent being. An independent mineral kingdom emerged because not everything that takes shape in a round is suitable for absorption into the higher stage of the plants. It was separated off. Now, I ask you please to see this process in its full significance. At that time, human beings were shaping their vegetable substructure. If in the second round we had had all the substances that were formed during the first round, we should never have attained to a higher plant structure. During the second round, as human pitris, we did something that was eminently egotistical. We told ourselves, as it were, that we would take from the soup what could be useful to us, and would leave behind what was no good for our further evolution. In the pitri-culture we threw out the mineral kingdom. We evolved higher at the expense of the mineral kingdom.

Then, in the third round, we threw off the plant kingdom as a being in itself. That is when the plants first came into being. We sucked in everything we needed in order to form our systems in such a way that we could develop kama and receive a blood circulation. In this way we raised ourselves into the animal kingdom and pushed down other beings into the plant kingdom. We won through to the animal kingdom in the third round. The animal kingdom of that time, however, cannot be compared with any form that exists today.

We have evolved to human beings during the fourth round by extracting, in very egotistical fashion, what we could use out of the animal kingdom. We discarded the rest, and this discarded element became the present animal kingdom.

Thus we evolved initially into mineral beings during the first round. We discarded the mineral kingdom during the second round, the plant kingdom during the third round, and the animal kingdom during the fourth. What are the minerals, plants, and animals? Minerals, plants and animals are evolutionary elements of our own nature that were once bound up with us, and were expelled. Everything we couldn't use we gave over to the Earth to evolve independently. When we survey the animal kingdom, we find it to be the same as what was discarded by us, that was still one with us in the third round. Now the occultist says: What you see as the animal kingdom is not something separate from you; it is something that in the third round was still inside you and reigned in you. You have shaken it off during the course of the fourth round. The rage of the jackal, the cunning of the fox, are your kamic elements. The fox has been created from the cunning that was in you; your rage created the jackal. Thus the whole animal kingdom is your own kama-world. You yourself have shaped and created the animal world. What has become physical today in the animal kingdom were the processes in your own kama-body during the third round. Look at the animals, and you see your own past. We have attained these stages by leaving others below us. Thus even now we purchase a higher stage of perfection by pushing others back. Every ascetic buys his own perfection by pushing another human being into an all-the-more blind rage of the senses. This is an eternal necessity.

All evolution advances ever forwards and forwards. The mineral kingdom, which was fashioned during the first round, evolved independently during the second and third round, and in the fourth round has taken on the forms we know today. It will no longer exist in the fifth round; it will scatter at the end of the fourth round, will fall away, as the bark falls away from a withered tree. In the next round, the fifth round, the lowest kingdom will be the plant kingdom; in the subsequent round, the animal kingdom; and in the seventh kingdom only man will still exist.

As *form*, the mineral kingdom has reached the highest level of development. It doesn't matter what substance it has. Through the transformation of the scattered forms it will receive another structure and constitute the archetype of a new cosmic system. By the end of the seventh round, the human kingdom will have dissolved. That is what happens when matter goes through its normal evolution. We have purchased every kingdom by casting off the previous one. In order for human beings to become what they are, they had to cast off from themselves the mineral, plant and animal kingdoms. We are now a little way past the middle of a *kalpa*, a cosmic age. Evolution in the second half will entail the re-absorption of what we previously cast off, and elaborating it at a higher level. This has to happen with the animal kingdom, the plant kingdom, and the mineral kingdom. In the animal kingdom we have as though spread out before us a great tableau of our passions.

When we tell a fable, we can transpose into the animal kingdom an astral process taking place in ourselves. We can thus have a tale about actions in the animal kingdom, but we are telling about our own passions. And when we tell a story about the overcoming of a passion in an animal, we are telling a story about overcoming a passion in ourselves. For the occultist it is clear that when he speaks about his own body, he is speaking about what he himself has formed, for we have shaped our bodies only during the fourth round. At present we are living in kama, and encounter the battle of kama with manas. When we look up to higher levels, we are preparing a higher ethical development. When our thoughts are associated with lower kamic levels, we are inwardly akin to the animal level of the third round.

The occultist says: The human world is maya. My tale is far more truthful if I leave illusory human bodies aside and relate the action using characters from the animal world. Human beings have their physical body thanks to the total evolution of the macrocosm. But the kamic human being has remained behind in the totality of evolution. If you do something that can no longer be made good, your body does not correspond with what you are. The macrocosm would demand that man stand at a higher level. What overcomes the body to the extent that it corresponds completely with the macrocosmic image, is depicted in the hare who sacrifices his physical body in external fire, and on the other hand evolves further.

Lecture 6

BERLIN, 30 SEPTEMBER 1904

The Mysteries of the Druids [30]

OUR medieval tales—Parzival, the Round Table, Hartmann von Aue—depict mystical truths in an esoteric form available to everyone, although they are usually only understood in their external meaning. What is their origin? We must look for their origin in times before the spread of Christianity. What was living in Ireland, Scotland [and in Scandinavia] was absorbed organically into Christianity. We are led to a particular centre from which this spiritual life emerged. The spiritual life [of Europe] spread out from a central Lodge in Scandinavia, a Druid Lodge. Druid means oak. This is why it is said externally that the ancient Germanic peoples received their instruction under the oak trees.

Druids were primordial Germanic initiates. In England [the Druid Lodges] continued to exist until the time of Queen Elizabeth I. Everything we read in the Edda or can find in the ancient Germanic sagas, can be traced back to the temple of the Druids. The composer [of these sagas] was always a Druid priest. The sagas are not merely some kind of symbol or allegory—they are this too, but are also something else.

Let's take an example: We know the myth of Baldur; we know that Baldur is the hope of the gods, that he is killed by the god Loki with a twig of mistletoe; the god of light is killed. This whole myth has a deep mystery significance which every individual who was initiated had not only to learn but to experience.

In initiation into the mysteries of the Druids, the first act was called 'going to see the corpse of Baldur'. It was thought that Baldur was always alive. Going to see him entailed gaining complete enlightenment on the nature of the human being. Baldur was man in his lost state. At one time there were no human beings like those of today, but different ones who were not differentiated, were not pushed down to the point of experiencing passions, who still lived in subtle, rarefied matter—Baldur, the bright human being. A proper understanding will see a higher meaning in these things which appear to us as symbols. This human being who is not submersed in what today we call matter, is Baldur. He lives in each of us. The Druid priest had to look for this higher man in himself. What this differentiation consisted of was explained to him, from the high to the lower levels of human development. The secret of all initiation is to give birth in oneself to the higher self. What the priest underwent more rapidly is what ordinary people will undergo over long sequences of development. For these priests to become leaders of ordinary people, they had to receive this initiation. The human individual who has descended more deeply must now overcome matter, and attain that higher condition once more. This birth of the higher self takes place in a certain way that is similar in all the mysteries. One has to re-enliven that part of one's human nature that has sunk into matter; one has to undergo a series of experiences—real experiences that cannot be like any sensory experience on this plane.

The stages [of initiation]: At the first [stage] one was brought before the so-called Throne of Necessity. One stood before an abyss; one really experienced in one's own body how things live in the lower kingdoms of nature. The human being is mineral and plant, but the present human individual cannot experience this; he cannot experience what the elemental substances experience, and yet the iron necessity, the imperative element in the world derives from the fact that we are also minerals and plants.

The next stage led the individual to everything that is living in the animal kingdom. One had to see, seething and churning together, everything that lives as passions and desires. The individual had to see this because the purpose of initiation is to look behind the scenes of world existence. People do not realize that what swirls through astral space is only concealed because of their physical sheath.

The veil of maya is a real covering, and one who is initiated must see behind it—the veils fall away and the individual sees clearly. This is a special moment: the priest becomes aware that [the veils] have held back instincts which would be terrible if let loose.

The third stage leads to a perception of greater nature. This is a stage which, without the proper preparation, is still very hard for the individual to comprehend. The fact that tremendous occult powers lie here, and that cosmic passions express themselves in these nature forces, is something that makes the individual aware that forces exist that he experiences on more than one occasion like his own sorrow (*die er nicht einmal so erlebt wie sein eignenes Leid*).

The next trial is called 'being given to the snake' by the hierophants. The effects produced from this are explained in the myth of Tantalus. The grace of sitting [like Tantalus] in the council of the gods can be misused. It signifies a reality which raises the human being above himself certainly, but it is associated with dangers that are not exaggerated in the curse on Tantalus. As a rule, a person would say they can do nothing against the laws of nature. [The laws of nature] are [creative] thoughts. With a thought that is just a shadowy brain-thought, one can do nothing. In a creative thought which builds and constructs the things of the world, in a productive and fruitful [thought], we have, instead of a passive [thought], one that is permeated with spiritual force. The empty chrysalis of a caterpillar is just the shell of the caterpillar; the living caterpillar is permeated by [productive] thought. Active, creative forces were poured into the empty-chrysalis thoughts of the priest, so that he became capable not only of perceiving the world, but of acting upon it as a magician. The danger here is misuse. At this stage the occultist gains a certain power through which he is in a position to deceive even higher beings. He must not only repeat truths, but experience them; he must decide whether something is true or false. This means 'being given to the snake' by the hierophants.

Just as there is a physical spine, so there is also a spiritual one which determines whether one receives a spiritual brain or not. The individual undergoes this process in the [third] stage of initiation, ['entry into the labyrinth']. He is lifted out of kama and provided with a spiritual spine in order to be lifted up into the vortices of the spiritual brain. The convolutions of the labyrinth are the same on the spiritual plane as the convolutions of the brain [on the physical plane]. The individual gains entry into the labyrinth, into the convolutions within the higher plane.

He then had to swear to silence; a bare sword lay before him and he had to swear the strongest possible oath. This meant that he would keep silent about his experiences before anyone who was not initiated as he was. These things, which are genuinely secret, cannot be communicated just like that. But it was possible for [the initiate] to compose myths in a form that would express what is eternal. Being able to express oneself in this fashion, one naturally had great power over one's fellow human beings. An individual who gives form to such a myth impresses something into the human mind. What we usually talk about is quickly forgotten, and only the tiniest fraction of it survives death. Eternal truths survive death the longest. Very little of the lower sciences survives death. But what is eternal survives, and appears again in a new incarnation. The Druid priest spoke from a higher plane. If his tales were the expression of higher truths, albeit in simple form, they penetrated deep into human souls. He had simple folk before him, but the truths penetrated into their souls, and they thus absorbed something that would be born again in new incarnations. In those times people heard fairy-tale truths. So today we have a prepared spirit-body; and if we understand higher truths today, it is because of this preparation.

Thus this period, which came to an end in the year 61CE,[31] had prepared the spiritual life of Europe, had provided the ground on which Christianity could grow. The [Druid] teachers continued to exist, and if we look, we can still find access to what was taught in these Lodges.

After the Druid priest had sworn his oath on the sword, he had to drink a particular drink, and from a human skull. This signified that the human individual had grown beyond the human element. This was the feeling the Druid priest had to have with regard to his lower body. He had to feel what lives in the body so objectively, so coldly, that he regarded it only as a vessel. Then he was initiated into the higher mysteries, and when he ascended into higher worlds [he met the living] Baldur. He was taken into a gigantic palace covered with gleaming swords. A man came towards him who threw seven flowers into the air—[the seven planets]. [The one being initiated saw three seats on which were enthroned]: the space of heaven (*Himmelsraum*), Cherubim, the Demiurge. Thus he became a true sun-priest.

Many people read the Edda without realizing that it is a telling of what really took place in the ancient Druid mysteries. There was a tremendous power in the hands of the ancient Druid priests, a power over life and death. It is a truth that everything becomes corrupted over time. Druidism was once most high, most holy. By the time of the spread of Christianity a lot had degenerated, and there were many black magicians, so that Christianity was like a salvation.

Only a study of these ancient truths can illustrate almost all occultism. In a Druid temple one stone was never placed upon another in the way done today, but according to exact astronomical measure; doors were built in accordance with measurements of the heavens. Druid priests were builders of humanity. A faint copy of this is preserved in the ideas of the Freemasons.

When we learn to see through astral material, we see:

The Sun at Midnight: 1st initiation.
Being given to the Snake: 2nd initiation.
Entry into the Labyrinth: 3rd initiation.

Lecture 7

BERLIN, 7 OCTOBER 1904

The Legend of Prometheus [32]

IN our last session I tried to show you how initiation took place in the Lodges of the ancient Druids. Today I should like to discuss a related subject but one that may perhaps seem to be rather remote. But from its depths we will see how we are able more and more to gain an understanding of our human evolution.

You have seen from my Friday lectures[33] that the legends of different nations have a profound content, and that myths are an expression of deep esoteric truths. Today I should like to talk about one of the most interesting legends, a legend associated with the whole development of our fifth root-race. At the same time you will see how the esotericist can always go through three levels of understanding with regard to the world of myths and legends.

Myths live initially in one nation or another, and are received exoterically, externally and literally. Then a disbelief in the literal interpretation sets in, and educated people try to find a symbolic meaning in the myths. But behind these two meanings there are five other meanings, for every mythological legend has seven meanings. The third one is where you are in a position to take the legend literally again in a certain sense; but you must first learn to understand the language in which the myth or legend is composed. I'd like to speak today about a legend that is not so easy to understand—the legend of Prometheus.

You will find something about this in a chapter in the second volume of *The Secret Doctrine* by H. P. Blavatsky,[34] and will see what profound content is hidden in this legend. However, there are some things it is not always possible to say in printed writings. Today we will be able to go a little further than what is covered in *The Secret Doctrine* by H. P. Blavatsky.

Prometheus is part of the mythology of Greece. He and his brother, Epimetheus, were the sons of a Titan, Iapetus. The Titans were themselves the sons of the oldest Greek gods, of Uranus and his wife Gaia. Translated into [English], Uranus means 'heaven' or 'sky' and Gaia means 'Earth'. I would like to stress that Uranus in Greek is the same as Varuna in India. So, Prometheus is a Titan, the offspring, like his brother Epimetheus, of Uranus and Gaia. Cronos, or 'Time', the youngest of the Titans, had usurped the throne of his father Uranus and assumed power for himself. He was himself dethroned for this by his son Zeus, and thrown with all the Titans into Tartarus, the abyss or Underworld. Only the Titans Prometheus and his brother Epimetheus had been loyal to Zeus. They had stood at Zeus' side and fought against the other Titans.

Now, however, Zeus also wanted to destroy the race of men which was getting above itself. And here Prometheus became the defender of humankind. He contemplated how to give humanity something by which it could save itself and no longer be purely reliant on Zeus for help. So the legend tells us that Prometheus taught human beings how to write, and the arts, and particularly how to use fire. By doing so he drew the wrath of Zeus upon himself. Because of Zeus' wrath, he was chained to a rock in Caucasus, and for a long time had to endure great torment.

The legend goes on to tell us that the gods, with Zeus at their head, instructed Hephaestus, the god of blacksmiths, to make a statue of a woman. This female statue was endowed by the gods with all the properties that are the external ornament of humankind of the fifth root-race. This female statue was Pandora. Zeus caused Pandora to bring harmful gifts to humanity, beginning with Prometheus' brother Epimetheus. Prometheus warned his brother against accepting these gifts, but Epimetheus let himself be talked into it and accepted the gods' harmful gifts from Pandora. They were all scattered over mankind, and only one good gift was held back: hope. The other gifts were plagues, suffering for mankind. Only hope was kept back in 'Pandora's box'.

So Prometheus was chained to Caucasus, and a vulture gnawed constantly at his liver. He endured this. But he knows something that is the guarantee for his release. He knows a secret [35] that even Zeus himself doesn't know, but wants to know. Prometheus doesn't betray the secret, even though Zeus sends Hermes, the messenger of the gods, to him.

Now the legend tells of his remarkable release. It tells that Prometheus can only be released by the intervention of an initiate. And Heracles was just such an initiate—Heracles who had performed his twelve labours. The performance of these twelve labours is the work of an initiate; they are twelve initiation trials, expressed symbolically. In addition, it is also said of Heracles that he was initiated into the mysteries of Eleusis. He was able to free Prometheus. However, there had to be someone who would sacrifice themself and take his place; and this sacrifice was made for Prometheus by Chiron the centaur, who was half animal, half man. He was already suffering from an incurable sickness. [He was actually immortal, but sacrificed himself in order to be able to die.] He suffered death and thus Prometheus was freed. This is the outer structure of the Prometheus legend.

This legend holds the whole history of the fifth root-race, and mystery truths are truly contained in it. The legend was certainly told in Greece; but it was also depicted in the mystery centres, so that the student of the mysteries really saw before him the destiny of Prometheus. It was supposed to show him the past and future of the whole fifth root-race. You will only be able to understand this if you bear something in mind.

Anthropogenesis—becoming human in the sense that we have humans today—was first attained in the middle period of the Lemurian race. Humankind of that time was guided by great teachers and leaders whom we call 'sons of the fire-mist'. Humanity of the fifth root-race is also guided today by great initiates, but our initiates are of a different kind from the leaders of humanity at that period.

You now need to be clear about this difference. There is a great difference between the leaders of the two preceding root-races and the leaders of our fifth root-race. The leaders of those root-races were also united in a Lodge of the White Brotherhood. However, they had not undergone their previous development on our Earth planet, but in other arenas. They were already exalted, mature human beings when they descended to the Earth in order to teach humanity, which was still in its childhood, in its first stages of emergence, and to instruct it in the skills it needed. This period of pupillage lasted throughout the third, fourth and even into the fifth root-race.

The fifth root-race has its origin in a handful of people who were selected from the previous root-race. They were nurtured and developed in the Gobi Desert, and then radiated out from there over the Earth. The first leader to give this impulse to human evolution was one of the so-called manus,[36] the manu of the fifth root-race. This manu was one of those leaders of humankind who had descended during the period of the third root-race. He was one of those leaders who had not only undergone development on the Earth, but who had brought their advanced maturity to the Earth.

Only in the fifth root-race does the development begin of manus who are human individuals such as ourselves, who like us have evolved only on the Earth, who have developed from scratch, as it were, on the Earth. Thus we have individuals who are already exalted leaders and master personalities, and others who are endeavouring to become leader and master personalities, so that, in the fifth root-race, we have chelas and Masters who belong to earlier root-races, and chelas and Masters who have undergone everything that people have undergone from the middle of the Lemurian period onwards. One of the Masters who has the guidance of the fifth root-race is selected to take on the guidance of the sixth root-race. The sixth root-race will be the first one to be guided by a manu who is an earthly brother. The previous Masters, the manus from other worlds, pass on the guidance of humanity to an earthly brother.

The dawning of our fifth root-race coincides with everything we call the development of skills. The Atlanteans still had a completely different life. They worked in a completely different way. Their technology and skills were completely different. Only with our fifth root-race do technology and craft develop in the sense that we understand them. The most significant discovery was the discovery of fire. Be quite clear about this for a moment. Just think how much our extensive technology, industry and skills depend today on fire. I think technicians would agree with me when I say that, without fire, our entire technology would simply not be possible. So we can say: The discovery of fire was the fundamental discovery, the impulse for all the other discoveries.

Along with this we must realize that, in the period in which the Prometheus myth emerged, 'fire' was understood to be everything associated with heat. The cause of lightning was understood in this way. The causes of all warmth and heat phenomena were summed up in the term 'fire'. An awareness that humanity of the fifth root-race was under the sign of fire, was expressed initially in the Prometheus myth. And Prometheus is none other than the representative of the whole fifth root-race.

Epimetheus is his brother. Let's translate these two words: Prometheus in [English] means 'the fore-thinker', and Epimetheus means 'the after-thinker'. Here we have the two functions of human thinking clearly laid out: in the human engaged in afterthought, and the human engaged in forethought. A person engaged in afterthought is one who receives into himself [impressions of] the things of the world and then thinks about them. This kind of thinking is kama-manasic thinking. From a certain point of view, kama-manasic thinking involves first letting the world make its impressions on you and then thinking about them afterwards. Today, people of the fifth root-race think mainly like Epimetheus.

But, to the extent that a person doesn't let things that already exist influence them, but creates the future, is an inventor and discoverer, to that extent they are a Prometheus, a fore-thinker. There could never be any inventions if people were just Epimethean. An invention is made by a human individual creating something that doesn't already exist. It first exists in thought, and then the thought is translated into [external] reality; that is Prometheus-thinking. This Promethean thinking, in the fifth root-race, is manasic thinking. Kama-manasic and manasic thinking move side-by-side like two currents in the fifth root-race. Manasic thinking will gradually spread out more and more.

This manasic thinking of the fifth root-race has a particular characteristic. We can understand this if we look back to the Atlantean root-race. That race had a more instinctive thinking which was bound up with the life force. The Atlantean root-race was able to take seed-force and turn it into a locomotive energy. Just as, in deposits of coal, people today have a reservoir of energy which they convert into steam for the locomotion of their steam engines and heavy loads, so the Atlanteans had large stores of plant seeds containing energies they could convert into locomotive power, which drove the vehicles described in Scott-Elliot's booklet on Atlantis.[37] The mind of the Atlantean was still able to control living nature, seed-power. The mind of the fifth root-race can only conquer lifeless nature, the forces of becoming in stone, in minerals. Thus the manas of the fifth root-race is chained to mineral forces, just as the Atlantean race was bound to life forces. All Prometheus-force is chained to the rocks, to the Earth. Thus Peter [*petrus* (Latin) = rock] is also the rock upon which Christ would build. It is the same as the rock of Caucasus. The human being of the fifth root-race has to look for his development on the purely physical plane. He is chained to inorganic, mineral forces.

Just try for a moment to hold an overall perspective of what it means when we talk about this technology of the fifth root-race. What is it for? If you take an overall perspective, you will see that no matter how great and stupendous the results are when intellectual forces—the manasic element—are applied to the inorganic mineral realm, in the final analysis it is for human egotism, for personal human interests, that all these energies of fifth-root-race discoveries and inventions are used.

Start with the first discovery and invention, and go from there right up to the telephone, to our latest discoveries and inventions, and you will see that great and stupendous forces have been put to use for us through these inventions. But what purpose do they serve? What do we bring with our railways and steamships from distant lands? We bring food; through the telephone we clamour for food. Fundamentally it is human kama that demands these discoveries and inventions of the fifth root-race. Looking at it quite objectively, this is what we have to realize. We then also see how the higher human being, which is transposed into matter, is indeed chained to matter during the fifth root-race because his kama demands satisfaction within matter.

If you look at things esoterically you will find that the human principles [i.e. the human members-of-being] are related to very specific organs of the body. I will go into this subject more deeply [later on], but today I will just mention which organs our seven human principles are associated with.

To begin with we have the so-called *physical principle*. This has an occult association with the upper part of the human face, with the root of the nose. Human physical structure, which began at one time—before this the human being was just astral and then structured himself into the physical—originated from this portion [of the face]. The physical body originated from this point and first structured the root of the nose, so esotericists recognize the root of the nose to be attributed to the actual physical-mineral element.

The second is *prana*, the body of the etheric double. Esoterically this is associated with the liver. The liver has a certain occult relationship to prana.

Then comes *kama*, the astral body. This developed its activity in the formation of the organs of nutrition, which are symbolized in the stomach. If the astral body did not have the very particular characteristics that it has in the human being, this human apparatus for nutrition, with the stomach, would not have the specific form it has today.

If we look at the human being, firstly in his physical foundation, secondly in his etheric-double body, and thirdly in his astral body, we have, as we can see, the foundation that is chained to what constitutes the mineral fetters of the fifth root-race.

Through the higher bodies, human beings raise themselves up from these fetters and ascend to a higher level. *Kama-manas* works its way up once more. Human beings liberate themselves once more from the foundation provided purely by nature. Thus there is an occult connection between kama-manas and that by which the human being is raised up and cut free from its basis in nature. This occult connection is the one between lower manas and the so-called umbilical cord. If there were no kama-manas in the human form, the embryo would not be cut free from the mother in the way it is.

Passing on to *higher manas*, we find it is occultly associated in the same way with the heart and blood.

Budhi has an occult connection with the human larynx, with the pharynx and larynx.

And *atma* has an occult connection to something that is dispersed throughout the whole human being: namely, to the akasha contained within us.

These are the seven occult relationships. When we look at them, the most important ones to emphasize for our fifth root-race are those with the etheric-double body and kama. If we also bear in mind what I said earlier about the Atlanteans' control of prana—life-force is what permeates the etheric-double—we will be able to say that in a certain sense the Atlantean was at a lower level. His etheric-double body still had the original relationship to all ethericity of the external world, and he was therefore able to control the prana of the external world. Because man has ascended one stage higher, the work has gone one level lower. This is a law: that when there is an ascent on one side, there must be a descent on the other. Whereas man previously worked out of prana on kama, he must now work out of kama onto the physical plane.

You will now understand how profoundly the Prometheus myth symbolizes this connection. A vulture gnaws at Promethus' liver. The vulture is a symbol of kama; it is actually really devouring the forces of the fifth root-race. The vulture gnaws at man's liver, at this foundation, and thus this force of the fifth root-race gnaws at people's actual life-force because man is chained to mineral nature, to the *petrus*, to Caucasus. This is how man had to pay for his similarity to Prometheus. For this reason, man must conquer his own nature so that he is no longer chained to the mineral element, to Caucasus.

Only those who emerge during the fifth root-race as human initiates can bring liberation to fettered man. Hercules, a human initiate, had to get to Caucasus himself in order to free Prometheus. Thus the initiates will raise man from his fetters, and what is in decline must sacrifice itself. The human that is still connected with his animal nature must sacrifice himself: the centaur Chiron. Man of the past must be sacrificed. The sacrifice of the centaur is just as important for the evolution of the fifth root-race as is its liberation by the initiates of the fifth root-race.

It is said that future prophesies were made for the people in the Greek mysteries. But what was understood by this was not some vague, abstract narrative of what was supposed to happen in the future, but an indication of the paths that conduct humanity into the future; what people have to do in order to develop into the future. And the human strength that had to be developed was portrayed in the great mystery drama of Prometheus.

In the three successive generations of gods—Uranus, Cronos, and Zeus—we have to picture three successive guiding beings of man. Uranus means 'sky' and Gaia means 'Earth'. If we go back beyond the middle of the third root-race, the Lemurian race, we do not find a humanity like the one we know today, but a humanity that *The Secret Doctrine* calls 'Adam Kadmon'.[38] This was a humanity that was still asexual; a humanity that previously did not belong to the Earth, had not yet developed the organs for earthly sight, that still belonged to the Uranian element, to the sky. Man arose through the marriage of Uranus with Gaia, and descended into matter and thus slipped simultaneously into time. Cronos—*Chronos*, 'time'—becomes the ruler of the second generation of gods from the middle of the Lemurian period into the beginning of the Atlantean era. The guiding beings were symbolized by the Greeks initially as Uranus, later as Cronos, and then they passed over to Zeus. Zeus, however, is still one of the leaders who did not undergo their schooling on Earth. He is still one who belongs to the Immortals, as indeed all the Greek gods still belonged to the Immortals.

The task of mortal humanity during the fifth root-race is to stand on its own feet. This humanity is represented by Prometheus. It was the first to introduce human arts and skills and the primordial skill of fire. Zeus is jealous of it because initiates of its own are growing in humanity who will take the leadership into their own hands in the sixth root-race. But humanity must first pay for it. Thus its primordial initiate must first take all the suffering onto his own shoulders.

Prometheus is the primordial initiate of the fifth root-race, the one who is not only initiated into wisdom but also initiated into action. He goes through all the suffering, and is freed by one who steadily matures in order gradually to release humanity and lift it out of minerality.

Thus mythology depicts the great cosmic truths for us. This is why I said at the beginning: One who ascends to the third meaning can take the myths literally once more.[39] In the Prometheus myth we have the vulture eating his liver. This can be taken quite literally. The vulture really eats at the liver of the fifth root-race. It is the battle of the stomach with the liver. In every person during the fifth root-race this Promethean battle of suffering is repeated. What is expressed here in the Prometheus myth is to be taken quite literally. If this battle did not exist, the destiny of the fifth root-race would be completely different.

So there are three meanings in myths: firstly, the exoteric and literal meaning; secondly, the allegorical meaning, the battle of human nature; and thirdly, the occult meaning, where a literal interpretation comes into play once more. Thus you can see that all these myths—at least all those that have a meaning of this nature—originate from the mystery schools and are nothing less than a rendering of what was presented in the mystery schools as the great drama of human destiny. Just as I was able to show you that the myth of Baldur in the Druidic mysteries was nothing less than a presentation of what took place in the inner sanctum of those mysteries, so in Prometheus we have what was experienced by the Greek mystery pupil in the inner sanctum of the [Greek] mysteries in order to gain strength and energy for life in the future.

Lecture 8

BERLIN, 14 OCTOBER 1904

The Myth of the Argonauts, and the Odyssey

By looking at various myths, I should like to create a basis for a certain kind of esoteric teaching that I will discuss in the following sessions. Today I should like to speak about a very important myth we also find in Greece, and which, like every other myth, can be interpreted in different ways and at many different levels. Today we will explore its essential core. Before I do so, however, I would like to preface it with some theoretical matters.

In the last issue of *Lucifer-Gnosis*,[40] I pointed out that within the last three cultural periods of Atlantis, a certain influence had begun in humanity which in a certain sense still continues today. This influence is associated with the fact that people became mature enough at that time to live in what we call our intellect, our reason. Prior to this man was more of a memory being. Up until the fourth Atlantean cultural epoch his memory was particularly highly developed. Our combinating intellect, our computing capacity, in short, that which is the basis of our whole present culture, began in the fifth Atlantean period, with the Proto-Semites. For this reason these Proto-Semites could also become the ancestral race of the whole fifth post-Atlantean root-race. During the course of evolution, the task of this root-race was to develop especially the intellect focussed on the physical plane.

Now, when a new phase of development begins in humanity, such as that of the intellect, it is possible that new beings, who had previously gone about their existence in concealment, start to have an influence on evolution. And indeed, from that point onwards, from the fifth Atlantean cultural period onwards, a certain host of beings, who had previously gone unnoticed, could [now] become active in the field of human evolution. You must picture these beings as highly developed, as far more highly developed than man at his stage of evolution at that time. But they had fallen behind, in a certain sense, from the beings who in the middle of the Lemurian era had begun to work on the human race. What happened now was an 'extra stimulus' (*Nachschub*). The beings I am talking about belonged with their whole nature to what we call the lunar development [Old Moon]. They had undergone their evolution during the Moon epoch but had not advanced as far as the beings that were able to intervene during the Lemurian period. They had fallen behind the normal development on [Old] Moon. They had come just far enough that they saw the capacities man had attained at that time as being equal to themselves, and the consequence of this was that they were able to take possession of them. Previously, people had not been intelligent beings; now they received the intellect. And this new capacity was used by these beings for their further development. And so it happened that the developmental phase began, which we call the preparation for objective 'scientism'. This had not previously existed and will cease to exist later on. All the wisdom achieved in human evolution was fundamentally connected with what we call love. Cold, purely calculating scientism is influenced by the beings representing an 'extra stimulus'.

So the influence of these beings, who are still active today in a certain way, will only come to an end when all our intellectual activity, everything we can know, everything we call rationality, is permeated once more with love. When intellect and love have united once more into a higher wisdom, then the influence of these beings who are invisible on the physical plane, will disappear. Making people aware of this influence, making the mystery pupils aware in the first place—this was the task of the Greek mysteries.

A particularly important period began for these beings around the eighth century before Christ. If we look at the cultural epochs of our fifth root-race—those that founded the ancient Vedic culture, then the ancient Persian, [then] the Chaldaean-Egyptian cultures—we find that even in the periods that brought forth the Druidic culture there was actually no objective, sober science. This only arose when the fourth cultural epoch began to dawn more and more. We can place the beginning of the fourth cultural epoch at around the eighth century before Christ. With this an objective science, separate from all the other human content of our heart and mind, began to dawn. When a Chaldaean priest engaged in astronomy, he was still trying to fathom the intentions of the rulership of the cosmos. It was the same with the priests of the Egyptians, and the Druid priests: they were looking for insight into the intentions of the cosmic ruler. Knowledge that was purely intellectual first dawned in Greece. This purely intellectual knowledge—which was prepared for gradually, and emerged through the influence of the beings I mentioned, but was still connected with other human activity—was unleashed completely in the fourth cultural epoch of the fifth root-race. In contrast to external wisdom, the initiates who received instruction in the mysteries of that time experienced the primal wisdom human beings had previously partaken of as something that had been lost, and needed to be found once more. There was a particular point in time when this deceased wisdom separated off from encompassing primordial wisdom. This point in time in which sober, dry wisdom separated from the comprehensive primordial wisdom was designated by saying: Around the eighth century before Christ, the sun passed through the spring equinox in Aries [the Ram]. This passage of the sun through Aries is a repetition of a passage that had taken place millennia before through the same sign. As is well known, the sun passes through the whole zodiac, through the zodiacal signs of Aries, Taurus, Gemini, Cancer, Leo, Virgo and so on, and so has passed through Aries many times before. The last time it passed through Aries [at the spring equinox], was when man still possessed the union of love and knowledge, and therefore also primordial wisdom. This primordial wisdom had now been lost and given way to an external culture of the intellect. This whole process in its occult significance was given expression by the Greek mystery priests through the tremendously profound myth of the Argonauts, in which a ram symbolizes the union of love with knowledge.

Let's first look at the myth as a whole. We are told that Phrixus and Helle suffered much at the hands of their evil stepmother Ino. Because of this, Phrixus' divine mother Nephele appears to him and advises him to take his sister and flee. Nephele gives him a large ram with a golden fleece, on which they can fly over the sea. Helle falls and is drowned in the sea, which is thereafter given the name Hellespont. Phrixus, however, arrives with the ram at Colchis. There he sacrifices the ram to Zeus, and gives the skin to King Aeëtes, who hangs it on an oak in front of a cave. Later, the Greek hero Jason, together with the most significant initiates of Greece at that time—Orpheus, Theseus, Hercules, and others—sets out to bring back the ram's skin from the barbarian peoples of Colchis. By gaining King Aeëtes' youngest daughter, Medea, for himself, it becomes possible for him to bring the ram's skin back to Greece. Before doing so he must conquer two fire-breathing oxen. He also has to sow dragon's teeth from which spring up fully armed warriors wanting to fight. Through Medea he is able to divert the battle. It was also she who enabled Jason to get the ram's skin and set out with it and herself on the journey home to Greece. Medea had brought her brother with her, and killed him, throwing him in pieces into the sea in order to delay her father. While the lamenting father gathered up the pieces, they were able to continue their flight to Greece.

In the eight and ninth century before Christ—in other words, at the beginning of the period of Greek civilization—the occult meaning of this myth was taught to the Greek mystery pupils. The occult meaning told there is that those beings who make use of people's dry, sober intelligence attained a particular significance from this time onwards. A longing for the primordial civilization that had once existed the last-time-but-one when the sun passed through Aries, awoke once again. The fact that the [Geminian] twins Phrixus and Helle are taken to Colchis by a ram [Aries], signifies nothing other than that a preceding sub-race, the Persian and Iranian civilizations with their Geminian nature—they stood under the sign of good and evil, Ormuzd and Ahriman—wished to win back the union of knowledge and love. The previous sub-race had taken this into hidden regions. Earlier, in the Atlantean period, this fleece, this wisdom, was the common property of human civilization; then it was taken into remote mystery schools. It had to be brought back. We thus see the rationale for the mystery schools of Greece expressed in the myth of the Argonauts.

In the Atlantean race there existed a primordial wisdom, so we are told. This primordial wisdom was at that time the common property of humanity. It was then lost, and could only be found in the caves and crypts of the mystery schools. But the Greeks re-established the mysteries for their initiates, and Theseus, Orpheus, Hercules and others became the founders of these schools of wisdom by bringing back to Greece the primordial wisdom. Through Thales, Anaximenes, Socrates[41] and other philosophers, a cold intellectual wisdom was introduced that is objective. Mystery wisdom is connected with love. It is a wisdom that cannot be attained without purifying the passions, the forces of kama. Intellectual knowledge, on the other hand, can be attained without purifying kama. Thus the very important legend of the Argonauts portrays for us the transition from the third to the fourth cultural epoch of our present root-race. The transition consists in a split in the previously common current of human culture into two streams: into mystery wisdom and into external intellectual knowledge. One of these streams was hidden, but in a way that was still effective and exerted an influence on Greek art and culture; it is portrayed in the return of the ram's skin. It was only on intellectual knowledge that it was henceforth to have no influence. That is the myth of the journey of the Argonauts.

In the legend of Odysseus we also see its relation to the transition from one race to another. The Odysseus myth has been successively analysed and interpreted in a great number of ways. Today I would like to discuss only the framework of the myth. In my book *Christianity as Mystical Fact* [42] I have tried to use the second kind of interpretation, the allegorical one. Let's look today at the third kind of interpretation, the occult interpretation.

Odysseus, who was one of the warriors at Troy, helped the Greeks to conquer Troy through cunning and cleverness. He went through great wanderings on water—I would ask you to keep this in mind. He came to the Cyclopes, overcame the chief Cyclops with his one eye, and travelled on to Circe who, as we are told, changed his companions into swine. Then he descended into the Underworld where he met the heroes who had fallen in the Trojan War. He was then subjected to the power of the Sirens, who lead men astray through the magic of their singing. We are further told how the majority of his companions succumbed to their temptation, and how he was saved by having himself tied to the ship. Odysseus then comes to a place between Scylla and Charybdis, where ships run the danger of being destroyed. He has to save himself from a whirlpool. He then comes to Ogygia, the island of the nymph Calypso. He remains there for seven years, and is released when Zeus orders Calypso to let him go. He finally arrives at Ithaca, his home. He is led by the goddess Pallas Athene to his house and to his wife Penelope who has had to withstand many perils from the suitors who are vying for her hand. She wove a cloth during the day, and undid it again during the night, because she had promised her hand to a suitor when the cloth was finished.

Now I would ask you to go with me through this outline of the Odysseus legend in the way we know it from Greek mystery wisdom. The initiation schools, where what is here related actually took place, led the pupil on the astral plane and the mental plane in such a way that he was able to move along a certain segment of human evolution—the segment from the middle of the Lemurian period to the point in Greece where the individual in the initiation schools founded by Orpheus, Theseus, Hercules and others, could find the primordial wisdom once more. So the pupil was led to the astral and mental plane, and was shown processes humanity had gone through from the middle of the Lemurian period up to the point when the Trojan War took place. A piece of the primordial wisdom is depicted for us by the mythical element in the journey of the Argonauts. It indicates that it existed side by side with science at that time.

What was it that was shown to people, to the initiation pupils, in the myth of Odysseus? This is portrayed for us representatively in Odysseus himself.

Let's go back to the middle of the Lemurian period. Man was making a transition at that point from a hermaphrodite state to a state of sexuality, a transition from a state of vision without external physical sense-organs for seeing, to sight with external physical eyes. Until the middle of the Lemurian period, man really did have 'one eye', which was then replaced by his two, external, physical eyes. The pupil was taken back into this phase of evolution. He was to experience the transition from the pre-Lemurian period to the post-Lemurian period, to the period after the middle of the Lemurian race up to the emergence of the external eye. The Cyclopes were people of the pre-Lemurian period. Odysseus encountered these on the astral plane. After this period the human astral body was lowered into matter that was becoming increasingly dense and solid. This was presented to the initiation candidate. Then we approach the first Atlantean times. The Atlantean gains more and more the ability to manipulate life forces, to use them for his particular ends. The Atlantean developed high, well-trained astral capacities, which a Greek could only see by transporting himself back on the astral plane. This was the time, spoken about in so many old occult writings, when the Atlantean generations fell into the wildest arts of black magic. This period was presented dramatically to the mystery pupil in images of transformation. It was a period when human passions were so distorted by forces of black magic that their astral bodies resembled lower animals. This was also the picture presenting itself when the Turanians[43] succumbed to these wild magical arts later on. The astral body was so transformed under the influence of black magical arts that, put symbolically, we can say: Circe changed Odysseus' companions into swine. The Greek initiate went through this point in human evolution.

Then Odysseus descended into the Underworld. Now, whenever a descent into the Underworld is portrayed in Greek mythology, it signifies that an initiation is taking place. When we are told that a hero descended into the Underworld, it is an expression in the narrative of nothing less than that the hero in question was initiated, that he became acquainted with things that lie beyond death. Odysseus was an initiate, and the legend of the Odyssey is itself a depiction of his initiation.

So now we move on to the moment when, after the Atlantean flood, people encounter the first effects of the beings I have been speaking about, who reveal themselves in civilization, in the knowledge and arts of those times, with effects that, after the Atlantean flood, had an influence on the intellect. The first beginnings of a purely external physical civilization were presented to the initiate as the lure of purely earthly arts, of purely earthly culture. These are the Siren calls of the young fifth root-race. The Siren calls of the young fifth root-race are what is so frequently spoken about in occult writings. For, on the one hand, we have the great wisdom-teachings of Manu, who indicates to the people of the fifth root-race that their intellect must be lifted up to the divine. This found expression in the Vedas, and in the religion founded and bequeathed to his religious companions by Zarathustra in Persia. Next to this we have a purely rational civilization which diverts people away from what develops under the influence of Manu. You will find what took place here written about in all occult writings. Manu chose a small handful of people and went [with them] into the Gobi Desert or Shamo.[44] Only a small number remained loyal to him while the others became disloyal and dispersed in all directions. This important event—that Manu initially chose a portion of the Proto-Semites, that only a smaller part of these chosen ones followed him while the other part perished because they followed the Siren calls of external culture—this important event was shown to the initiation candidate.

The Odysseus myth then goes on to portray another important moment in human development: the passage between Scylla and Charybdis. So what is actually beginning now in humanity? Now comes the first beginning, as we have seen, of actual kama-manas culture. Up to this point it had been in gradual preparation. Now it begins. Our fifth root-race is a predominantly kama-manasic civilization. Kama is active at the astral level, and continues to be so in our astral body. Manas, however, is what is active in the physical brain. Only in a future phase of evolution will kama, the astral body, also be so far advanced as to be able to think. Today manas has established itself initially in the physical brain. Between these two hurling vortices, Scylla and Charybdis, we have to pass. This is depicted by Odysseus' passage between Scylla-manas and Charybdis-kama. On the one side is the astral whirlpool, the drives, desires and passions in which man can founder, and on the other side is the physical intellect chained to the rock. We have already met the rock in the Prometheus myth. Now we meet it again. The human intellect is exposed to all the dangers of the body, the rock. Man has to pass between the cliffs of the physical intellect and the whirlpool of astral life. If he gets through, if he recognizes what dangers threaten him but nevertheless manages to stand firm, he comes to the island of Calypso, to hidden wisdom. There he can look out into the future of humanity, undergo a period of trial lasting seven years. This is also why Odysseus remains with Calypso for seven years. Everyone who wishes to attain initiation must go through a trial period of seven years, and this is indicated by the stay with Calypso, where hidden wisdom lies behind the illusions. Only then can he come to the place the soul reaches when it has escaped the whirlpool of astral passions. Read Homer's *Odyssey*; he indicates that man seeks his own soul. The return of one's own soul: that is the searching for home. Anyone wishing to really understand *The Odyssey* should not take the view of a recent researcher who suggests that what is meant by Polyphemus and the Cyclopes is nothing other than that Etna had spewed out fire, and the burn mark on the giant appeared to Odysseus to be his eye!

Odysseus finally reaches home as a beggar with no outer possessions. This implies that the individual who has seen through the unimportant aspects of the external world and worldly possessions, who seeks the soul's home not in maya but behind maya, reaches home in a mystical sense as a beggar. That Odysseus is in truth a sage, is indicated by Pallas Athene leading him home. In all esotericism one's own soul is portrayed as a feminine being. A female figure is always chosen as a symbol for the striving of the soul. Goethe calls it the Eternal-Feminine. Just as in the journey of the Argonauts we have Medea, so here we must regard Penelope as Odysseus' own soul, to which he seeks the way back. In the Christian religion it is the Virgin Mary who is the human soul striving for redemption, but the significance here is much more profound. This Penelope, to be precise, is the soul of man of the fifth root-race. The fifth root-race has to cultivate the intellect. In itself it is the most unproductive thing; it can only become productive when applied to a content. The intellect is a net spun around things we have got from somewhere else. When external experience teaches you something, you can then encircle it with what is spun by the intellect. When higher occult wisdom teaches you something, you can then encircle it with what is spun by the intellect. People often say that occult wisdom contradicts intellect. Nothing contradicts intellect. But intellect only exists to combine, to join things. Out of itself it can obtain nothing; you can't prove anything from the intellect. This unproductive quality of the intellect, which is actually the soul of the fifth root-race, is depicted in Penelope's constant spinning and undoing of her weaving. Odysseus is led by wisdom. The initiate has to find the way to the soul of the fifth root-race, to the unproductive intellect. But he will only connect with the soul of the fifth root-race in the right way if he is led by Pallas Athene. Pallas Athene in turn is feminine, a goddess, another force in the soul—Wisdom, the real guide. After many journeys—and provided they are genuine journeys of development—man must attain the intellect. Pallas Athene, Wisdom, must be his guide in this. This is what was presented to the mystery pupil in Greece, and what Homer wished to relate in his profound legend of Odysseus.

So what is portrayed for us in the legend of Odysseus is an initiation as cultivated in Greece at that time, an initiation that was nothing less than a repetition at the astral and mental level of the experiences of people in the Lemurian period up to the time of the mysteries themselves. Odysseus is cunning and clever, and Troy is conquered by his faculties. The clever man of intellect is man of the fifth root-race. But he must seek his home, his Penelope, by detours, in order properly to walk his path in the fifth root-race. One who is merely cunning or clever would not find the right path in the fifth root-race. He must first get out of himself and broaden his view by looking back over the long path of humankind's evolution. Odysseus is the representative of the cunning kama-manas individual who must make many journeys in order, in the fifth root-race, to be led back to his soul.

LECTURE 9

BERLIN, 21 OCTOBER 1904

The Legend of Siegfried

WHEN we try to form a living picture of the emergence of the Nordic mythological world, the period before the first Christian century and thereafter is of particular importance. At that time the northern regions of Europe were in a state of expectation. The event, whose outworking was expected to spread over Europe—the descent of the divine father-spirit into a human physical being—was known to the initiates of the northern peoples; it was also foretold in the mysteries.

In the ancient Druid mysteries of the North, similar initiations were performed as those among other peoples on the ascent at that time. But a difference needs to be highlighted between what was in preparation in the North and what was occurring in other regions. To get some idea of this for ourselves, we need to cast our gaze back to the emergence of the human races in the regions of the Earth that were gradually becoming the habitations of people. It is only possible to speak of a physically habitable Earth from the Lemurian root-race onwards. But this Lemurian period was preceded by an etheric Earth, to which the myths of Paradise refer, as well as the mythologies of the various peoples of the northern and southern parts of the Earth. They are what constitute the mysteries' treasures of wisdom. Schooling in the mysteries, depending on people's level of understanding, consisted of gradually revealing to them what the human soul was capable of absorbing and working on. So we can speak of the mysteries having a common origin that lies in the imaginative and inspiritive knowledge of its guiding teachers, and therefore also of the unity of the teachings; but also of the differences that have arisen through the course of time and geographic and human environments. They were protected by the most stringent obligation of silence—because in premature hands, evil would result instead of good—and betraying the mysteries to premature people incurred the penalty of death.

Let's shed some light on what were the common principles underlying the ancient Atlantean mysteries, which emerged from the oracle centres as schools of initiation. Based on neo-Platonic sources and on Plotinus, the chronological research in theosophical literature follows the accepted view that in Socrates we have the historical moment at which the wisdom previously inspired by divine beings, and that used man as its instrument, descended into man, into the *anthropos*, and gradually became his property, his task, his duty. Socrates still had to suffer death for passing on truths from the mysteries to his pupils. He accepted the death sentence willingly and consciously. But the metamorphosis of this idea—of a consciously experienced death that really leads then to true life—had first to ripen in the northern peoples. They were prepared for it slowly and gradually by what was living in their own mysteries, and were brought to a greater level of maturity in their soul organism through a long period of waiting. Buddha was expelled from his religious community because he went out, wandered from place to place, and brought people the teaching of liberation through death. This was a mystery truth not yet allowed to be taught. It could only become valid in a far distant time, and at present could only live in single fire-souls who were preparing this future time. It would only find its fulfilment in Christianity. But until that time of fulfilment, certain peoples had to receive a training in their mysteries which, as the substance of the nation, predestined them for the far-distant tasks of human civilization.

We were preceded by four root-races; we are the fifth root-race, the post-Atlantean race. The names given to the first sub-races—or cultural epochs—of this post-Atlantean time can be translated into [English] approximately with the words: the sub-races of the Spirit, the Flame, and the Stars. The first sub-race, the Race of the Spirit, was given the content of the fifth root-race in spiritual form by

Manu; it encompasses the Indian people. The second sub-race is the Race of the Flame, which was given a religion by Zarathustra. The third sub-race was the Race of the Stars, that of the Chaldeans, Babylonians, Assyrians, from which the Israelite tradition later emerged. The Greco-Roman peoples, who have their first chief representatives in Greek and Roman culture, were the fourth sub-race. This is the one in which Christianity first took root in Asia Minor, Greece and Rome. It was destined to be the one most strongly influenced by Christianity, but it was not yet able to grasp its significance which surpasses the capacity of human comprehension. A long preparation was needed for this. This was provided by the sagas in the Nordic mysteries, which lived on in song and epic, and were carried in rhapsodic form from land to land, and intensified to religious ardour.

Our fifth root-race received Christianity, founded at the beginning of our time reckoning, as something passed down to us. But a few centuries before Christianity was brought to the northern regions, and even in older times, the ancient Druid initiations existed. They continued to exist until roughly the point when it was clear that the twilight of this preparing Celtic culture had begun. You must bear in mind that all the influences that had affected other peoples had not reached these northerly regions. All the currents that were part of the Race of the Flame and the Race of the Stars had not penetrated as far as these northerly regions. In the North something had remained of the remnants of Atlantean culture that had been brought across by initiates. Woden [or Odin] was the initiate of the northern peoples who had brought the elements of Atlantean culture into these regions.

Everywhere in these northerly regions it was Druidic initiation that was practised. I have already related that one of the founders, we could even say the chief founder, of these initiation centres, was called Sig or Sigge. And something happened here in these northern regions that was similar to what happened later in Palestine at the founding of Christianity: Sig surrendered his body and gave it into the service of a high individuality. This is why the changed Sig was later called Odin. Odin was the bearer of the spiritual culture at this time. Thus Sig was the chela in the North who placed his body at the disposal of the higher, more spiritual Odin. He lived on later as an initiated master. Sig is a very special case. After the beginning of Christianity, he could not start a movement in the way the Master Jesus[45] had done. Sig has to lead this northern culture, which had established itself here, to its downfall. He is called upon to lead the northern peoples up to the point where Christianity reaches them from the South through the fourth sub-race of the fifth root-race. The ancient chela Sig is the one who must lead the northern peoples into their tragic doom. This is why he is also called Sigurd, which means 'the one who leads into the past'. *Urd* is the Norn of the past. *Fried* means the same as 'that which leads to peace', in other words to death, to demise. This is preserved in the [German] word *Friedhof* (= graveyard), 'that which is led to death'. The same chela who had prepared the way for the great initiate had to lead northern culture to its demise. Its spiritual content declines and is replaced by advancing Christianity. What I have just said was the content of a prophecy which was described in the later mysteries of the northern peoples in the following way: We have to be a people that is lead to peace. This is what sounds out in the various mysteries of these northern peoples. The whole course of future events written in the texts from primordial times, was proclaimed in the northern mysteries, and what later became the content of the 'Song of the Nibelungs' and the legend of Siegfried, arose from these prophecies. The second part of the 'Song of the Nibelungs'[46] depicts the completion of the Nibelungs' karma.

I need to mention a peculiarity that always occurs in a situation like this in the development of humanity: before a new phase sets in, there has to be a brief repetition of the previous phase of development. This repetition of previous phases is particularly evident here in the North. It shows us how what had been occurring in the North since Lemurian and Atlantean times had to be overcome before these northern peoples would be sufficiently mature to develop themselves up to the Christianized fifth root-race. The one in whom the sum total of northern culture's history lives, is the initiated Siegfried.

So let's look briefly at the main points of the Siegfried saga.

At the beginning we are presented with the life of three heroes—Gunther, Hagen, and Giselher—at the court of Worms. We then hear how the hero Siegfried woos Brunhild on Gunther's behalf. We hear that at the court in Worms, Siegfried is regarded as an exceptional personality. And indeed he is, for he is invulnerable; he has killed the possessors of the Nibelungs' treasure horde, has made his whole body hard as horn from his battle with a dragon, and has won the cloak of invisibility. So he has two attributes always evident in initiates of pre-Christian times: they are invulnerable, and they are unrecognizable. They are invulnerable due to their initiation. In the Gospel it says: There are three that bear witness: blood, water, and the Spirit.[47] Blood and water have to be conquered. It was blood and water that made [the initiate] invulnerable in the times preceding Christianity. But these initiates always had a spot where they could be wounded. Achilles is the depiction of an initiate in earlier times. He was dipped in the River Styx and was vulnerable on his heel. Siegfried was dipped in the blood of the dragon and was vulnerable between his shoulder blades. An initiate can make his true nature unrecognizable because he possesses the cloak of invisibility; this makes the possessor of higher occult faculties imperceptible to the external world. The owners of the Nibelung treasure had these occult abilities. They originated from the Atlantean race, and it was especially the initiates of the Atlantean root-race that had these capacities. But they were also present in the initiates of the fifth root-race, and thus Siegfried had them too. When Siegfried slew the dragon, he came into possession of the Nibelung treasure hoard. So what is this Nibelung treasure? It expresses the fact that the Nordic peoples provided the ground and soil, so to speak, from which the fifth sub-race could emerge. The fifth sub-race is also called the race of great discoveries and inventions, which conquers the whole physical plane and becomes great in possession of the external world. It ought to possess, on the one hand, and transform this possession into wisdom, on the other. We should see in the Nibelung treasure nothing other than a linguistic mutation of the ancient word *Nifelheim*, Nebelheim ['the place of mists', from German *Nebel* = mist, and *Heim* = home]. It is what was known in the North as the physical Earth, the

Earth at the moment it started to become physical. What this preparatory race had spread out around it, and what Christianity encountered in it, is solid possession. The gold of the Nibelung treasure is earthly possession, the representative of earthly possession. This is something the initiate possesses, and what he is allowed to possess, because he can keep watch over it in the appropriate manner.

Now, you all know how the Siegfried saga continues in this old version. It is not the oldest version of the saga, but is the one that concerns us. As is known, Gunther then woos Brunhild of Iceland. Siegfried twice overcomes Brunhild in combat. Gunther strives for her hand, but Siegfried, armed with the cloak of invisibility, fights invisibly at Gunther's side, and Brunhild believes that it is her suitor Gunther who has won in the combat against her. Siegfried is glad that she becomes Gunther's wife. But now, in a moment of weakness, Siegfried's wife Kriemhild betrays the secret to Brunhild, that in reality it was the invisible Siegfried and not Gunther who conquered her. Brunhild is outraged and plans to kill Siegfried. But she must first discover *how* he can be killed. For this she wins over Hagen von Tronje, who lives at the court.

Hagen is a figure we know from the ancient Druid mysteries. Hagen is an important name of ancient Druid initiates. He is an initiate who represents the highest streams of spiritual life lying in the past, which come to expression in the fact that what went before always opposes what comes afterwards and does battle with it. Siegfried belongs to the subsequent stream, immediately preceding Christianity. Hagen belongs to the preceding Druid stream. Thus Hagen is brought in to destroy Siegfried. For this to happen, Kriemhild has to betray that Siegfried is vulnerable on a particular spot. The meaning of this spot here becomes clear. Kriemhild reveals that Siegfried is vulnerable between his shoulder blades, and precisely on the spot where the cross has to be carried. He doesn't have the cross yet. Christianity is still absent in these ancient peoples. On the spot where the cross will rest in order to be carried through the world—that is where Siegfried is vulnerable, so the Siegfried saga tells us, because Christianity is not yet present. Siegfried, who leads the Sig initiates to peace, to rest, is vulnerable on the spot where

Christianity later makes [people] invulnerable. He is overcome by residual powers from previous cultures. Hagen, the representative of previous streams, kills him. This is a depiction of the previous Nordic culture being succeeded by the fifth sub-race. The meaning of this succession is shown in the Siegfried saga.

So what is it that these Nordic races are actually fighting against?

In paving the way for Christianity, they fight against all the old elements that have remained behind from the Atlantean period. They have to defend themselves against these constantly. The soul of the Nordic peoples must defend itself against what still assaults it from the remnants of Atlantean culture. It is an earlier layer of culture that protrudes here into the fifth cultural epoch. But those who have remained behind in Atlantean culture are an impediment to further development, and must be fought.

Later battles are depicted in an older version of the Gudrun saga.[48] Here we encounter the soul of the Nordic peoples in Gudrun. She fights against the great initiate of the Atlanteans, against Attila or Atli or Etzel, who comes from a remnant of an Atlantean race, the Turanians, and approaches from Asia. The historical Attila and his people were also called 'the scourge of God' by the Europeans. Attila was an initiate with very significant occult powers who fought at the head of his tribes. This is why it is right to say of the battles with the Huns that the hordes fought in the air. For anyone who knows and understands these things, it is clear what this is about. Attila didn't retreat from anything he encountered in Europe. He only retreated voluntarily from the Pope, the representative of Christianity, for he was fully aware that he could do nothing against the representative of Christianity. The Nordic peoples knew they had to defend themselves against influences from the East; but these were unable to harm Christianity.

Now, the later Nibelung saga tells us that Kriemhild made a plan to take revenge on those who had killed Siegfried. She takes revenge in a way that connects her with Atlantean elements. She manages to recruit Attila's hordes; she becomes the wife of the Hun king, Attila. After the death of Siegfried, she had lived for a while at the Burgundian court. She had come into possession of the Nibelung hoard, and had used it as a great benefactress. But her enemies, who originated in previous epochs and were represented in Hagen, sank the Nibelung treasure into the Rhine. Kriemhild kept to her plan of destroying her old Nordic enemies with the help of Attila. By Kriemhild's plan, the Nibelungs are enticed down to Attila's court, and on the way they encounter precisely those spirit-forces that were to succeed them. At the Danube they meet Christianity in the form of Rüdiger von Bechlaren and his wife Gotelinde. Here is the dawning glow of Christianity, that which was to take the place of the cultures of the North-European peoples. The Nibelungs meet their downfall; they are murdered at the Hunnic court. Although she gets her revenge, Kriemhild also meets her own downfall. And how does this happen? She, who is the transformed Gudrun, the folk-soul of Nordic culture, associates herself with Atli-Attila-Etzel, the Atlantean, and takes revenge on the representatives of her own culture, who had killed an initiate. She herself dies.

If you only look at the saga aesthetically, you will naturally ask: How is it that at the end Dietrich von Bern, Hildebrand and all the other heroes, who belong to a layer that has already converted to Christianity, are introduced to the Hunnic court? After all, they are Christian heroes already. Christianity brings death to the old folk-soul; it overcomes the old folk-soul. This is not something that was inserted into the saga later on, but something that had lived as a prophecy in the mysteries long before the emergence of Christianity. These events were a theme in mystery initiation. It is not only initiation into the truths of the present that are part of mystery initiation, but also those of the past and the future. An apocalyptic element was always a part of it. The Siegfried saga had been the apocalypse of the northern peoples for a long time. This saga is not a poetic invention somehow emerging out of the people from separate pieces, as is imagined by philologists. The people don't write poetry [of this nature]. Only someone who has no idea how things happen in the soul of a people could say such things. The sagas are nothing other than depictions of what took place in the crypts of the mystery centres. What is contained in the saga is nothing other than a portrayal of mystery processes. Such a process, for which in the South they had the word *mysterium*, was called a *maere* in the North, from which our word *Märchen* [= fairy tale] later arose for the lesser processes. '*Uns ist in alten maeren wunders vil geseit*' (In ancient tales many wonders are told us).[49] 'Wonders' is no less than a 'sign', a sign for things seen as happening on higher planes.

Norse mythology is so interesting because it portrays something that cannot be found in any of the southern mythologies. What the southern peoples portray in their myths always signifies an ascent; they have always received and adopted something that leads to a higher stage. The Indian, Persian, Babylonian, Chaldean peoples, and those which succeeded them, also have tragic figures, to be sure—just recall the Chronos myth—but the tragic element is most developed in the North because the peoples there had to wait a long time. It was a culture of preparation that lasted a long time, with a high form of initiation which—and this is the important point—was a culture that descended so far that the initiate was a human being. The initiate of India was a bodhisattva, then they were rishis; later, among the Greeks, the initiates were sun-heroes such as Hercules and Achilles. Only once the ladder of initiates had descended so far did the initiated human individual appear here in the North, who was lacking only one thing: namely, that which is Christ, the Man-become-god. We encounter the man of the North in an attitude of waiting. He is vulnerable on the spot where Christianity must establish itself.

So we have four 'layers' to take into consideration:

Firstly, Woden. He runs parallel with what was developing in the South in the first sub-race of the fifth root-race.

Secondly, Odin.[50] He runs parallel with the second sub-race of the fifth root-race.

Thirdly, Baldur, the sun-hero. He runs parallel with what developed in the South as the Babylonian-Chaldean-Assyrian epoch. But what is an ascending culture there, is a waiting culture in the North.

[And fourthly,] initiates of the waiting culture expressing the element of tragedy. Because the old forces are coming to an end, we see the tragic death of Baldur and the tragic death of Siegfried.

Lecture 10

BERLIN, 28 OCTOBER 1904

The Trojan War

SINCE we have a few newcomers here today, I should like to mention briefly that I have tried in the course of these sessions to show how various myths and legends have an esoteric content, and that one just needs to be able to sort out the language of these myths and legends to find, in some cases, profound esoteric truths in them. Today I should like to speak about one of the legends that have the peculiarity of being a legend on the one hand, but on the other hand have a completely external content derived from the physical plane; in other words, they express a very specific physical event.

Before I speak about this legend, I would like to mention a fact most of you are already aware of, but which we need to impress upon ourselves again and again. It is this: that during the course of our fifth root-race—so in the period from the downfall of Atlantis in the fourth root-race to the next root-race—a great step was taken in the whole evolution of humanity: namely, that leaders of humanity, the manus, arise out of humanity itself. All the great manu leaders, who had advanced humanity in the previous root-races, who gave it its great impulses, had not undergone their development purely on the Earth but in part on other heavenly bodies, and had thus brought to the Earth from other worlds the great impulses they had to give to humanity. The manus of the Lemurian and Atlantean races, and also the original manu of our fifth root-race, are super-human individualities who underwent on other planets their great schooling whereby they could become leaders of humankind. By contrast there are individuals during our fifth root-race who become so highly developed within humanity itself that they can become leaders of humankind from the sixth root-race onwards. And the chief leader of the sixth root-race will be a human being just as we are, but one of the most advanced, or *the* most advanced of all human beings. He will be a being who began his development in the middle of the Lemurian period when humanization in general began, but was able to progress more quickly, and participated in all the stages of human evolution. This will be the fundamental nature of the manu of the sixth root-race. The chief manu of the sixth root-race and all those at his side must pass through initiations of the most varied kinds; they have to have been initiated many times over. Thus from its beginnings there had always been initiated individuals in the fifth root-race, individuals who were initiated in the direction, so to speak, that they could walk the path of their own free will. Throughout the whole of the Lemurian period, and also during Atlantean times, this had not been the case. Those who had helped the progress of humankind at that time, who governed and guided it, who were the leaders of states and the leaders of large religious communities, were under the influence of higher beings. During the Lemurian and Atlantean period they were directly dependent on those more highly developed beings who had undergone development on other planets. Only in the fifth root-race is humanity liberated more and more. Here we have initiates who are associated with higher beings, to be sure, but who are not given such broad and fully worked-out advice; the initiates of the fifth root-race are given increasingly more freedom in [working out] the details. The initiates are indeed given directives, impulses, but in such a way that they carry them out using their own mental-spiritual capacities and judgement.

Our fifth root-race has seven sub-races. They arise as follows in the course of development.

The first sub-race is the Race of Spirituality, of the Spirit. It is the race from which Indian culture originated, the culture of the rishis, the Vedic culture.

We then have the second sub-race, the Race of the Flame; this is Persian civilization that finds its expression in the religion of Zarathustra.

Then we have the third sub-race, which we call the Race of the Stars, the original Chaldeans, of which the Israelites are a major branch.

The fourth sub-race is the cultural group from which the Greeks and Romans emerged, the Race of Personality.

The fifth race is the Race of the World; this is the one we ourselves are in, the cultural group of the Germanic and Anglo-Saxon peoples, which at present is in a phase of development, and which makes people into free personalities; it is the race that conquers the [physical] world. It will be succeeded by the Slavic sub-race, a cultural group coming up from Asia.

I spoke in my last lecture about the great initiates of the Nordic regions. I mentioned that symbolic terms were used for an initiate or for someone with some kind of connection with initiations, and one symbolic expression was that the initiate was *invulnerable*. This invulnerability, which we meet in Siegfried, is also found in Achilles. Indeed, there is a profound esoteric meaning in the myth involving Achilles. You must bear in mind that what I have described takes place gradually in the course of the fifth root-race. The manu had arranged the leadership of humanity at the beginning of the fifth root-race in such a way that it was completely under the care of the priesthood who received their inspirations directly from higher divine beings, from super-human beings. It could even be left to these priests to categorize the people. It would have been impossible in any culture other than one led by priest-rulers to divide people justifiably into castes. Thus we find a caste system actually only in the real priest cultures, in Ancient India and in Ancient Egypt, where initiated priests were at the top, who did not follow kamic impulses but higher instruction. They acted impersonally, kama-free, and it could be left to them to undertake the serious business of dividing people into castes, which in Egypt and India was originally fully justified. If you look at these castes you find the whole plan for the development of the fifth root-race incorporated in them.

This plan is that the guidance, the leadership, of the fifth root-race is gradually moved from a priestly cast of mind to a worldly one, from the priest to the king. A worldly king who was not a priest would still have been an absolute impossibility in the early stages of the fifth root-race. In the Atlantean period when people did not yet receive their impulses from the thinking intellect but from other forces, and even still at the beginning of the fifth root-race, the guidance of humankind had to be kept away from any worldly powers and left to those who received divine inspiration. Thus you find in Indian and Egyptian civilization a pure rule by priests. The priest is the regent, the source of everything. The priest belongs to the highest caste. Warriors, who have a purely earthly occupation, belong to the second caste. Then it goes down to those who farm the land.

It was intended that these castes would gradually become independent. In what develops in the flow of time we never have what is really externally present in space. Please note this. If a spatial relationship is to become temporal, this happens in a ratio of four to seven, in such a way that the four-ness expands into a seven-ness. The four castes, juxtaposed in space, come to temporal expression during the course of the fifth root-race so that we see seven sub-races gradually developing to independence. The ratio of four to seven is based on a very particular law. Today I will just say about this that the seven sub-races develop in such a way that in the first sub-race we essentially have exclusive rule by priests, in the second root-race, we have rulership by priest-kings and magi. Zarathustra, the true magus, is the advisor of the priest-king. During the third root-race, rulership can be transferred to worldly kings who still follow the advice of priests. Only during the fourth root-race do we have worldly kings who are no longer in relationship with priestly power. The first worldly kings appear initially among the Greeks, and Greek dominion becomes more established through worldly kings.

The expansion of Greek civilization is depicted outwardly—in legendary form—in the story of the Trojan War. This legend of the Trojan War is no less than the mythical depiction of an esoteric truth, namely the blossoming of the fourth root-race and the supersession of the final phase of priestly rule by purely worldly rule. This is indicated right at the beginning of the legend of Troy in an exceptionally subtle way.

You know that in esotericism matter is everywhere portrayed by the symbol of water. Water is the esoteric symbol for matter. I need only point to a theological example: In the Nicene Creed, where it says '...suffered under Pontius Pilate,' it should actually say 'suffered in Póntos Pyletós,' [51] which means 'in compressed water'. The Son of God descended to suffer in the matter present on the physical plane. In the Christian Credo, *póntos* was Latinized into *Póntius*, and *pyletós* into *Pilatus*.

When Thales says everything has arisen from water, what he means by this, in truth, is all-encompassing physical matter. We are dealing here with water as physical material. Physical material will be the yardstick for those who assume the guidance of humanity—the worldly kings. Previously there had only been kings who had a connection with the divine. Peleus is the king who is to rule on the physical plane, drawing his power from the physical plane itself. In the mysteries this was depicted for the people in a myth, by telling them that Peleus married the sea-goddess Thetis. What we have here is the marriage of the guidance of humanity with the material of the physical plane. Thetis is the goddess of water, of the sea. And the offspring of this marriage is Achilles. Achilles is the first initiate of this kind. He is therefore invulnerable, except on his heel. All the initiates of the fourth sub-race are still vulnerable somewhere. Only at the end of the fifth sub-race will there be initiates so far advanced that they are no longer vulnerable. Achilles is dipped in the Styx—this means he has died in everything of an earthly nature and is caught up into a higher plane.

We have an important phase here in humanity's development. In the middle of the fourth sub-race, spiritual life descends, and we have initiates of the physical plane for the first time. And now something very special occurs. The previous world leaders had been kama-free, they were without [lower] desires; they had had to cast off everything of a kamic nature through the various levels of their previous initiations, up to the point of spiritual initiation. As long as there had been priests in the ancient sense of the word, it had been impossible for anything of a kamic nature to influence the rulership of the world. But kama brings about separation, kama makes it possible for people to turn against one another. There had been battles and conflicts before this too, but people had not yet progressed to the point of being able to contrast good and evil. We can't measure strife and war among the people of that time by our present yardstick; we must measure it with the same gauge as for the animal world. One couldn't say something was good or evil any more than we can say that a lion or a tiger is good or evil. Real evil first began when manas united with kama, and man was directed by kama. And this led to people fighting against one another consciously.

This is indicated in the myth by the fact that at the wedding of Peleus and the sea-goddess Thetis, all the gods are present, but one goddess is absent. Eris is missing, the goddess of strife, because humanity was still at a stage before kama united with manas, which gave rise to a separation by which people contrasted themselves with others. But then Eris appears; she throws an apple among the guests on which is written 'to the fairest one', in order to sow discord. This then led to the first war in the fifth root-race, the responsibility for which lay entirely in human hands. Only after this point is it possible to speak of people raging consciously against one another.

Everything else in the myth is an elaboration of what began here. The apple of Eris was to go to the most beautiful of the goddesses. The three goddesses, Hera, Pallas Athene, and Aphrodite, argue over the apple. These three goddesses signify different levels of soul life on the higher spiritual planes. But things are no longer to be decided on the spiritual plane but on the physical plane. Paris is therefore called upon to make his judgement from the physical plane. Here is the crux of the matter, where the essential point becomes tangible.

What results must ensue when decisions are made from the physical plane?

When manas first appeared on the physical plane, it mingled with kama. To be sure, people were kamic before this, but this did not have the significance of good and evil. But now manas united with kama, and people thus became conscious of their deeds. Manas entered into what is man's lower nature. He had attained his kamic evolution already on Old Moon. The coarsest kamic elements fell away from the Earth with the withdrawal of the moon, and now accompany the earth as its moon satellite. In esotericism, the moon is the leitmotiv, the marker, for our lower nature, for that which pulls us down, for where we could end up if we ourselves incline to our lower nature.

The ominous aspect of the union of manas and kama during the fourth sub-race is that man, who has to make decisions, connects himself with the kamic element, with the moon principle, with Selene.[52] The name Helena comes from Selene. In the association of Paris with Helena we have the marriage, in the fourth sub-race, of manas with kama symbolically expressed. Man on the physical plane has grabbed the moon principle to himself. You can find this everywhere in esotericism where 'moon' is spoken of. The result of this whole liaison being created directly on the physical plane in a conscious way between the manas-principle and the kama-principle, is war. The Trojan War is also a symbol of this fact. It really did take place; the most important events of the Trojan War were played out on the physical plane. But they also have a symbolic significance. The myth of the Trojan War has a mystical content, but the events also took place externally on the physical plane.

Now there is something else I would ask you to understand. When the fifth root-race has reached its end and the sixth root-race is on its ascent, an influence will have been developed in the area of the conscious intellect which at the moment, during the fifth sub-race, is still very much in the background but is nevertheless already in development. It is something that emanates from the musical element. The significance of music will come to expression more and more in the fifth sub-race. Music will not just be an art form but will be a means of expression for things quite different from what is purely artistic. There is something here that points to the influence of a very particular principle on the physical plane. The most significant impulses from the initiates of the fifth root-race will be given in the area of music or something similar to music. What has to flow into the fifth root-race, and particularly in the field of conscious intellectual life, is what we call kundalini fire. This is a force that is still slumbering in man but which will become increasingly significant. Today it has a great influence, great significance, in what is perceived through the sense of hearing. In the further course of development in the sixth sub-race of the fifth root-race, this kundalini fire will gain great influence over what lives in the human heart. The human heart will really have this kundalini fire in it. Man will then be permeated by a particular power that will live in his heart, so that in the sixth root-race he will no longer distinguish between his own well-being and the well-being of the whole. Man will be so permeated by kundalini light that he will have the principle of love as his innermost nature.

In the seventh sub-race, the majority of humanity will truly be in chaos, for the root-race will then be approaching its demise. But a small portion of people in the seventh root-race will be the true sons of kundalini fire. They will be permeated by all the forces of kundalini fire; they will provide the substance for the next root-race, for those who will direct the further evolution of humanity. Thus the fifth root-race steers its course towards the heights where divine fire, kundalini fire, ignites with pathos the divine principle in people's inner nature, so that one person will no longer be separated from the other, but rather, as far as the thinking intellect extends, a sense of brotherhood is brought about. This fire will live in people one day. And already, in those who are initiated in the course of the fifth root-race, there is living a hint of this divine fire in which exists the power of brotherhood, and which will supersede the separation between people. But it still has to work its way through, is only in its beginnings; it is still concealed, veiled by people's divisive passions, by the separating powers of kama. And on isolated occasions where it appears as the herald of a coming time, it takes on another form, a completely different character. On the plane of deception, divine fire is divine wrath. Only once brotherhood has suffused the whole of humankind will it be divine love. But it is divine wrath for as long as it appears as the fervour in a single individual; and it is a powerful force in the individual precisely because the rest of humanity is not yet sufficiently mature.

This is also expressed by the poet—Homer is called 'the blind poet' because he sees inwardly—in his work: 'Sing, goddess, the anger of Peleus' son Achilles'. This is the divine wrath that Homer speaks about right at the beginning of the *Iliad.* The *Iliad* is a depiction of kundalini fire expressed on the physical plane. In the quarrel between Agamemnon and Achilles, anger flares up as divine wrath. The legend of the Trojan War portrays how the old priest-king state is superseded by the rule of worldly kings. Troy is a state in which the king is under the influence of the old priesthood. This is superseded by the principle of worldly cleverness. It is a beautiful depiction of how worldly cleverness is victorious. Odysseus, the one of crafty stratagems, is victorious. He is the initiate of the fifth sub-race who received his initiation through his wanderings. The spirituality of the old priesthood is superseded by intellectuality. This is also expressed in the image of Laokoön being caught in the coils of serpents. The serpents, the symbol of worldly cleverness, ensnare Laokoön, the representative of ancient spirituality.

When you look at all this, you see that the legend of Troy preserves no less than a world-historic situation. Such events were presented in the mysteries. In the older mysteries preceding the Eleusinian Mysteries, precisely this important moment of the ascent of the fourth sub-race of the fifth root-race was depicted, among other things the Trojan War, which really took place, was depicted in the mysteries before it occurred. For anyone unfamiliar with theosophy, this is of course preposterous. But there is a principle in the mysteries that presents the future alongside the past. And because future events are anticipated, so must they also be kept secret. The mysteries did not exist to satisfy people's curiosity, and [only] those individuals could participate in them who were called upon to collaborate in working on the future in a transformative way. There they could gather the impulses for their task. This is the meaning of the mysteries.

So if someone were to reveal a mystery, this would mean telling people openly what was going to happen in the future. Doing this would inevitably cause confusion among their fellow human beings. Only advanced individuals receive the impulses for this. They have the task of slowly bringing people to where they one day need to be. Only a few advanced individuals, who are ahead of their fellows by perhaps five hundred years, are in a position to bear these secrets and to act in accordance with the mysteries. Just suppose others were to hear of this: they would want to bring things about immediately for which people are not yet sufficiently mature. Every mystery becomes common property one day, under substantially changed circumstances. Everything will be revealed at a specific time. The secret nature of these things lies in the fact that initially only a few individuals have the task of preparing the future; they must become the leaders in order to guide the others.

There are secrets today that can only be revealed in the sixth root-race, when completely different conditions of brotherliness, which cannot yet be realized, will be prevalent. Those who knew something about these things were naturally extremely anxious that, due to carelessness, something of the mysteries might be revealed. In earlier times, revealing the mysteries carried the highest penalty; in olden days this was the death penalty. It was not the priests who carried out the death sentence but people on the outside who had some knowledge but were not initiated. Fear of the mysteries being revealed led to the tragic end of many great individuals. Socrates too was the victim of such a judgement, although unjustifiably.

II

Richard Wagner in The Light of Spiritual Science

LECTURE 1

BERLIN, 28 MARCH 1905

MYTHS are stories told to people by great initiates, within which great truths are hidden. The Trojan War, for example, depicts the battle between the third and fourth sub-races of the fifth root-race. The third is represented by Laokoön, the priest of the ancient priest-state who was also the king, and the fourth by Odysseus, personified cunning, the power of thought coming into development in this epoch. In the North too we find development led by such initiates. In Wales there was an assembly of initiates of the pagan era, of priests, the highest blossoming of which was King Arthur and his Round Table. Alongside this was the union of the Holy Grail and its knights who laboured to proclaim Christianity.

Art, political development—everything is connected with the great initiates of these two groupings, the expression of pagan and Christian civilization. The influence of the Grail community became increasingly prominent around the turn of the thirteenth century. The period of town foundations was a particular turning-point in European civilization, when the old peasant culture based on land holding was succeeded by a bourgeois urban culture. This marked a decisive change in the whole way of life and thinking. It is therefore not without significance that, at the time of the *Sängerkrieg* (minstrel contest)[53] at Wartburg castle, we see a legend emerging, the legend of Lohengrin. What was it this medieval legend wished to portray?

Today we have no idea what the medieval folk-soul was like. It was particularly sensitive to the spiritual currents moving under the surface of things. Today we see the Lohengrin legend as representing a strong Catholic viewpoint. But although there may be things here that today disturb us, we need to consider that at that time the legend could only have an effect if it was clothed in a garment that really moved souls of that period. The clothing had to give the legend a fervent piety, so that it had something of what was living in the people. So, what did the legend signify? An initiation: the initiation of a chela to an arhat, of a pupil to a Master. A chela of this kind first became a 'homeless one'—this means, he carries out his duties like anyone else but must make the effort to see beyond himself and to develop his higher 'I'.

So what are the attributes of each stage of initiation for a chela?

Firstly: overcoming the personal element, the liberation of the god in his inner being. Secondly: freedom from any doubt; all scepticism ceases. The things of the spirit stand before his soul as realities. Freedom from any kind of superstition; he is able to test everything for himself, and so can no longer fall prey to deception. At a still higher stage he is given the Key of Knowledge. It is said of him that he receives speech; he becomes a messenger of the supersensory world; the depths of the spiritual world are revealed to him. That is the second stage of chelaship. The third stage is where, just as he says 'I' to himself, the individual is now able to say 'I' to all beings of the world, where he is lifted to the all-encompassing aspect of the All. The term used by mysticism for a chela at this third stage is 'swan'. He becomes a mediator between the arhat, the teacher, and the people. Thus the swan-knight is a depiction for us of a messenger of the great White Lodge. Thus Lohengrin is a messenger of the Grail community.

Civilization was to be given a new impulse, a new aspect. You know that in mysticism the soul or consciousness is portrayed as something feminine. So here too the consciousness of the new bourgeois culture is portrayed as a feminine quality. The appearance of this new culture is seen as a shift of consciousness to a higher level. The medieval soul is depicted in Elsa von Brabant; and Lohengrin, the great initiate, the Swan in the third grade of chelaship, brings the new culture from the Grail community. It may not be questioned. It is a profanation and misunderstanding to question an initiate about what has to remain secret.

Thus the upward shift into new states of consciousness always happens through the influence of great initiates. As an example of how these initiates operate, I should like to recall Jakob Böhme.[54] You know that Jakob Böhme proclaimed profound truths. He relates that, as an apprentice, he was left alone one day in his master's shop. An unknown man came in and wanted a pair of shoes. The boy wasn't allowed to sell anything while his master was absent. The unknown man said a few words to him, left the shop, and then after a while called the young Böhme out to him and said, 'Jakob, for now you are still small, but one day you will become a completely different person whom the world will be astounded by.' What does this mean? What we have here is an initiation; it portrays the moment of initiation. For some time the boy doesn't understand what has happened, but the impulse has been given.

A moment like this is also depicted in the Lohengrin legend. Legends of this nature hold important references only discernible by one who can see things in the greater context. The Lohengrin legend, as already mentioned, appears in association with the legend of the *Sängerkrieg*. Richard Wagner used it for his Lohengrin work. We see from this how high Richard Wagner's inner calling was.

Richard Wagner deals with another very ancient legendary theme in his *Ring of the Nibelungs*. It deals with an ancient Germanic legend concerning the fate of a people who, as a remnant after the great Atlantean flood, spread over Europe and Asia and ushered in the post-Atlantean epoch. The legends contain a memory of the great initiate Woden, the Aesir god. Just as all the Nordic gods are none other than great, ancient initiates, so Woden too is an initiate from the Atlantean period.

We can distinguish three levels in Wagner's work on the Siegfried legend. On the first level we find a contemplation of modern culture. For Wagner, people today have become the day labourers of civilization. He sees the great difference between people in modern times and in medieval times. Today the work people do is mostly machine work whereas in medieval culture all work was an expression of the human soul. Houses, villages, towns—everything in them was fashioned with meaning; people took pleasure in them. What are our warehouses, our shops, our towns for us today? What relationship do they have to our soul? In those times a house was the expression of an artistic idea. The whole streetscape, the market at the centre of the town with its cathedral that soared above everything else and to which everything was inclined, was an expression of the soul. Wagner felt this contrast. What he wanted to achieve in his art was to portray something that at least in one area showed the human being completely. A whole, harmonious human being, in contrast to the day labourers of industry, is what Wagner wanted to portray in his Siegfried. This is something our great minds have always felt. Goethe felt it; Hölderlin [55] felt it and expressed it like this: you see craftsmen but no human being; thinkers but no human being; priests but no human being; masters and servants, the young and the staid, but no human being. No turning back was possible externally; our whole development could not be reversed. Wagner therefore wanted a temple of art to arise in which the artistic work as a totality would lift people above their ordinary lives. Modern times especially needed such a place of upliftment, precisely because modern life was so fragmented. This was the first idea that occupied Wagner in his Siegfried work.

But a second plan came to him when he went down into deeper layers of his feeling. In the early medieval period an old legend had entered German literary work: The Wibelungs.[56] At that time the deepest sensibility of the folk-soul lived in a legend of this nature. Only by making a real study of the folk-soul is it possible to get an idea of what lived in people's hearts at that time. Such legends were the expression of deeply inward and great truths. For example, the legend of Charlemagne. What is reported about the emperor is not historical in the modern sense of the word; people looked deeper into the old circumstances. Here the Frankish kings became the ancient ancestors of the later post-Atlantean root-race. The Wibelungs were priest-kings who did not only take care of their realm but also gave it certain new spiritual characteristics. These legends were a memory of a great period now passed. In this respect Charlemagne's coronation in Rome [57] was seen as something of great importance. In very ancient times, the Wibelungs had been initiate priest-kings. A memory of this continued in the German kaiser legends. Wagner was led to these.

A particular figure seemed to epitomize for him the contrast between the new times of material property and the medieval period which still had a connection to that spiritual culture. This was the Barbarossa[58] legend, which he worked on. In Barbarossa too we see a great initiate. Legend tells of his crusade to the East; from the initiates there he was to bring back the higher wisdom, the knowledge, of the Holy Grail. The myth of the twelfth and thirteenth centuries has it that he was held by a spell inside his castle. His ravens bring him news of what is happening in the world. Ravens are an ancient symbol of the mysteries. In the mystery terminology of Persia they signify the lowest level of initiate; they are the messengers of the higher initiates. What was this initiate meant to bring? Wagner wished to depict the supersession of the old period by the new with its relationships of property. What had been alive earlier had withdrawn like Barbarossa.[59] The intervention by initiates crystallized for him in Barbarossa.

This idea still shines through in the 'Nibelungs'. At first understood externally, and now on a deeper basis, it becomes the expression of the profound view of the Middle Ages in which is portrayed the rise of a new civilization. But then, with an infinitely intuitive understanding of the old Germanic mythological gods, Wagner looks for an even deeper grasp of this idea, and instead of Barbarossa he finally chooses the figure of Woden. This [Germanic] mythology depicts the end of Atlantean civilization, the rise of the fifth root-race out of the fourth. This at the same time is the development of the intellect. The development of human intellect, of self-consciousness, did not yet exist in the Atlanteans. They lived in a kind of clairvoyance. Only in the fifth sub-race of Atlantis, in the Proto-Semites, did the first elements of a combining intellect[60] take shape, which lived on in the fifth root-race. And here an ego-consciousness begins to arise. An Atlanean did not say 'I' to himself with the same intensity as people of subsequent ages. This ancient culture was brought over after the destruction of Atlantis; Europeans are a later branch of the Atlanteans. So a contrast is now created between the general mental-spiritual culture and the initiates who work behind the scenes and inspire the external intellect.

The dwarves of Nifelheim are the bearers of ego-consciousness. Wagner places Woden—the old Atlantean initiate—and Alberich—the bearer of egoism, from the Nibelung race of dwarves, the initiate of the post-Atlantean age—in opposition to one another. In mysticism, gold is highly significant and meaningful. Gold is light; light that flows outwards becomes wisdom. Alberich brings gold, hardened wisdom, out of the River Rhine. Water is always the soul-element, the astral. The Ego, the gold, the wisdom of the 'I', is born out of the soul-element. The River Rhine is the soul of the new era in which the intellect, ego-conscious, arises. Alberich gets hold of the gold, seizes it from the Rhine maidens, the feminine element, who represent the original state of consciousness.

This situation was living deep in Wagner's soul. The emergence of ego-consciousness in this new era is powerfully felt, powerfully portrayed at the beginning of *Das Rheingold* in the chords in E-flat major. Musically this also lives and moves through Wagner's *Rheingold.* Wagner had literary works before him that had their origins in the ancient myths. Something was living in these legends which, full of life and energy, permeated the soul with spiritual rhythm. What we ourselves live and are, becomes awake; it sounds in these ancient legends and penetrates our being.

Lecture 2

BERLIN, 5 MAY 1905

We shall see in these lectures how the figures in Wagner's dramatic operas rise up to the gods and then descend again to the people, in order to depict in humanity its liberation and redemption.

Right at the beginning of *The Ring of the Nibelungs* we meet the whole leitmotiv of the fifth root-race, of the post-Atlantean age: the birth of the Ego, of self-consciousness, out of the astral element. Water, as you know, is the occult representative of the astral. If we wish to understand the mood that pervades Richard Wagner, we need to enter into the Norse myths. Without being aware of all the details, Wagner nevertheless expressed the power and symbolism of what is living in these myths. If we allow everything that is clustered around the Norse gods to work on us, we find that they have something tragic about them. Everything points to an ending: the Twilight of the Gods. What is this essential feature that led to such a wonderful work of art [as Wagner's *The Ring of the Nibelungs*]?

Let's picture what the Earth was like at the time of the original Nordic race. You would find a tropical climate, one that in no way plays second fiddle to the tropical climates of today. Humanoid apes, elephant- and giraffe-like animals lived in this region. Nature was very different from what it is today. This was gradually succeeded by the Ice Age, and we find our ancestors there with their primitive culture. Our Germanic culture emerged from the conditions after this Ice Age.

There were mysteries and mystery schools in the North as well. There were Druid mysteries, and very profound Druid mysteries more to the West. There was an initiate behind these: Odin. Remnants of these old Druid mysteries were preserved primarily in lands with a Celtic population. There were traces of it in England up to the time of Queen Elizabeth I. Then they ceased. The old Druid mysteries tell of a chela, Sig or Sigge, who, at a particular age, surrendered his individuality and became able to take into himself a higher individuality. This is a procedure that is described in all the mysteries. At the Baptism by John, Jesus also offers his body to a higher individuality. Everything connected with Sig recalls the mystery that a chela can give up his individuality for a higher being. Odin entered into Sig in order to prepare what was to take place in the future.

Every mystery pupil was taught that the world of the Norse gods would be succeeded by Christianity. All Odin's work is a preparation for the coming Christianity. In the wanderings of the Atlanteans towards the Gobi Desert, various tribes were left behind here in the North. While the age of the fourth sub-race unfolded in the South, something was also happening in the North. Here too there were four phases of development, the last of which was the Twilight of the Gods itself.

In the Norse myths we hear what course these four preparatory epochs took. During this period Odin was initiated four times to higher levels. In his first initiation, during the first sub-race, he hangs for nine days on the cross, on the wood of the World Ash. Then Mimir comes to him and teaches him the runes. Here too, hanging on the cross signifies a redemption. In the second initiation, he gains [a drink of the] mead of wisdom, guarded by Gunnlod in a cave. He has to turn himself into a snake in order to get into this subterranean cave. He stays there for three days in order to drink of the mead. In the third initiation, corresponding to the third sub-race, he has to sacrifice his own eye. This is the eye of wisdom of the legends, recalling the one-eyed Cyclopes who signify the people of the Lemurian race. This eye receded in us long ago. A hint of it is still visible in newborn babies. This is the eye of the clairvoyant. Why did Odin have to sacrifice it? In every root-race there is a short repetition of previous development. Thus in the third sub-race clairvoyance had to be sacrificed once again so that what lit up first in Odin—[namely] rational wisdom, the hallmark of the European way of viewing things—could emerge. Odin's fourth initiation is connected with Siegfried, the scion of the gods, the scion of Odin. Human initiates now take the place of a god for the first time.

Siegfried is initiated. He must awaken Brunhild, his higher consciousness; he must purify himself of his passions by walking through flames, through fire. In this way he undergoes purification, catharsis. He had previously slain the dragon, overcome his lower sensuality. Through this he has gained invulnerability; only between his shoulder blades is there still a spot where he can be wounded. The vulnerability of this spot points symbolically to the fact that this fourth sub-race is still lacking something that only Christianity can bring. One had to come who was invulnerable where Siegfried was vulnerable—[namely] Christ, who bore the cross between his shoulders, at the place where Siegfried could be killed.

Another onslaught, a storming in of Atlanteans, was to founder against Christianity. The tribes led by Atli[61]—Attila or Etzel—were of Atlantean descent. These Mongolian peoples retreat in the face of the Christianity they meet in the form of Pope Leo I.[62] The old culture is succeeded by Christianity.

In earlier times, evolution was depicted in myths in symbolic pictures. This is also the case with the Baldur myth. We have to recognize a Nordic initiate in [the figure of] Baldur. All the conditions of initiation are fulfilled here. The enigma of Baldur conceals a profound truth. The unique place of Loki in Norse mythology can only be understood through this enigma. You know that Baldur's mother, who was afraid [for Baldur] because of bad dreams she had had, gets all beings to swear not to harm Baldur. Only one unprepossessing plant, the mistletoe, is forgotten, and it is from this mistletoe, which had not sworn the oath, that Loki fashions an arrow. He gives [the arrow] to the blind god Hodur while the gods are playing at throwing things at Baldur [whom nothing would hurt]. Hodur throws the arrow at Baldur and kills him.

You know that the evolution of the Earth was preceded by another one: the [Old] Moon period. The substance of [Old] Moon was similar to living matter. A few of the Moon plants remained at that level, and intrude in a disturbing way into the subsequent world. They are unable to grow in mineral soil; they can only grow parasitically on other living things. Mistletoe is a Moon growth. Loki is a divinity of the Moon; he originates, at any rate, from the Moon period. He was perfect during the Moon period, now he represents what is imperfect, what is evil. Now we can also understand why Loki in Wagner's operas has a double nature, being simultaneously both male and female. As you know, unisexuality coincides with the separation of the moon from the rest of the planet. The new creation is presided over by the Sun-god Baldur. There is now a confrontation between the old and the new creations, between the Moon-realm and the Sun-realm, a clash in which Baldur, the representative of Sun culture, falls victim. Blind Hodur represents the blind necessity of nature living in the mineral kingdom. He had to take on guilt in order to make a certain progressive element possible. In the mysteries Baldur had to be brought back to life after being killed by Loki through Hodur.

These are feelings that imbue us when we follow the creations of Richard Wagner. Let's look at a scene in the *Rheingold*: the Rhine maidens are guarding the treasure of gold. The dwarf Alberich is burning with sensual desire for them. Then a passion for the gold awakens in him and he forsakes love because anyone who wants to possess the gold and power must abjure love. So he forges the ring. What is connected with this ring? Possession, egotism; as long as a person is not separated off, they want nothing for themself. Egotism begins when the human being is encircled by the ring of sensuality. Alberich has to forsake love; he, the representative of self-consciousness, surrounds himself with what is physical. The physical body is built according to the same laws that rule in nature, from which the Rhine maidens' gold is obtained. Egotism, separate existence, is bound to the gold. Gold here is wisdom gained through perception (*Anschauung*), not creative wisdom. In order to gain creative wisdom, the human being must first make himself receptive to it. Let's go back in time to when the human being had not yet divided into two sexes. At that stage he was not yet able to think, to create self-awareness for himself through thinking. Everything he created was created through love. The human being had to purchase his higher mentality at the cost of half his productive power, by becoming unisexual.

Where did all this come from? It all came from beings who were creative previously. The Earth had to pass through a transition into a different condition so that man could receive this solid corporeality. Odin belonged to earlier times, to the times of surging fire-mists. Where the purest fire-forces still reigned on Earth when the Spirit of God moved upon the waters—that is where Odin was at home originally. Now Odin had to transform his house into a solid fortress. The Earth had to solidify. Valhalla, the home of the gods, was built by the giants. These are the people of the Lemurian race, the Lemurian giants, who still lack a higher mental level. The giants—humanity wresting itself out of its bodily nature—demand Freya for this: once again a female figure. She symbolizes consciousness, the consciousness needed to preserve oneself, to rejuvenate oneself.

And now it is Loki who, out of the fiery element, is able to build something that is right for our lower nature. Loki relieves Odin from having to sacrifice Freya; Loki brings it about that Freya can remain with the gods. What must the human being attain? The ring—that which is our bodily nature structured according to certain laws. Passion, which is necessary for our sensual nature, must be given up for the sake of a higher love. Before the highest development can begin, the soul too must be built up. The giants relinquish Freya, relinquish love. Love remains with the gods. The giants content themselves with the ring, the element of gold, which comes with a curse. Love returns only through Christianity.

Norse mythology has a tragic character. We see that Odin is sorry to pass on his rulership to one born of the human race. He wishes to retain his governance and tries to win back the ring. Then he meets Erda. Erda is the spirit of the Earth, the consciousness of all humankind as long as it evolves on Earth. Her daughters, the Norns, know the higher consciousness of the Earth, they represent the primal knowledge of the Earth concerning its past, present, and future. They unravel individual knowledge; above individual knowledge is a consciousness that has the character of eternity.

Odin hands over the ring to the giants. The giants begin to fight amongst themselves. Separate existence leads to conflict, and thus an ominous motif enters in. This ominous motif expresses the transition of humanity, which had previously lived more in community, to a new humanity, to separate existence, to war against one another. Odin realizes his position towards humanity, particularly his relationship to the fifth root-race.

A rainbow leads from Valhalla to the Earth. The rainbow has a particular meaning in occult wisdom. You know the rainbow that appears after the Flood. Now we find this symbol repeated in the Norse myths. It symbolizes the transition from the Atlantean to the post-Atlantean era. In those [Atlantean] times, the air was much thicker and water much thinner than they are today. The form of precipitation we have today, rain, didn't exist. A rainbow wasn't possible at that time. The land where the Norse peoples emerged is not unjustifiably called the 'realm of mists' (*Nebelheim*), Nifelheim. It is from this 'realm of mists' that the water masses formed that deluged the continent of Atlantis. Only at the end of the Atlantean period, after the Flood, did the rainbow appear. Occult research tells us what this means. In the biblical rainbow of the Flood, and in the rainbow bridge of Norse mythology, we meet something that depicts the connection between man and the gods. When Odin is conquered by Siegfried,[63] it signifies that man now takes the place of the ancient gods. The task of the fifth root-race is prepared for, which involves allowing the leaders of humankind and the masters to emerge from humanity itself. The earlier leaders of humanity came down from higher worlds. Now it would be a Master who had gone through all the stages of humanity's evolution—only more quickly than other people—and, as a more advanced individual, leads humanity.

We will speak again about Siegfried and hear more about this development, next time. You will see that, in order to portray what moved humanity most deeply, Wagner used the power of the Norse myths. It is here that we find the immensely uplifting and penetrating quality of the Wagnerian operas.

LECTURE 3

BERLIN, 12 MAY 1905

IN the preceding lectures we saw how Wagner, the great artist, turns to mythology in order to depict the great interrelationships in the world. The whole content of the Norse worldview up to the time of Christianity is contained in the Siegfried legend. This Nordic worldview has a tragic strain: it ends in the Twilight of the Gods. What does this tragic strain mean?

I mentioned that there were also mystery centres in the North. Norse mythology ends with the Twilight of the Gods, and what this meant was explained in these centres to the pupils. In those mysteries a portion was revealed of what was still concealed and would come to pass only in future times. The priests of the Nordic world had to make known that the old world of the gods would decline and, out of the fire in which the Norse world would perish, a new world would rise up to a purified love through Christ. The old had to die. Hence the tragic quality towards the end. This is what shines through in Wagner's work in such a wonderful way, this preparatory mood in the Norse legends, which dies away in the Twilight of the Gods.

This Norse worldview has four phases. Humanity passed through four stages before the coming of Christ. Today we live in the fifth sub-race of the fifth root-race, which was preceded by others: by the Sanskrit civilization, then the Persian-Medean and the Chaldean-Babylonian-Egyptian civilization; the Greco-Roman cultural epoch was the fourth, and now in the North we have the Teutonic-Germanic peoples. Christianity pierces right into this with a new quality. At this stage everything will change and the old will die out. This is beautifully depicted in the story of Winfrid Boniface,[64] who cuts down the sacred oak. In the old mysteries, *oak* means the same as *Druid.* Thus the cutting of the oak means the destruction of the old Nordic religion. This victory over the Druid rites was prophezied by the Nordic mysteries.

While the four sub-races were developing in the south, the northern peoples had their own development. There too we have four phases; development goes through four stages the last of which is the Twilight of the Gods. It is curious how the whole previous development of humanity is repeated in these four phases. Humanity has been through various conditions. Norse mythology is a kind of memory of the whole history of the Earth. It lives in this mythology as a way of seeing things, as a mythical content. And these four stages of development are alive in Wagner's dramas because he derived them from these myths. Wagner was completely right to compose a tetralogy. These four parts, along with the preliminary evening, depict the evolution of humanity. Christianity will be the fifth stage.

What is the basic motif in the *Rheingold*? And what is the basic motif of our present root-race?

If we go back to the Polarean root-race, we find human beings who did not yet have self-consciousness and who were not yet split into two sexes. It was the same with the Hyperboreans. Only in the third root-race, in the Lemurian period, did man become unisexual. And only in the Atlantean period, in its fifth sub-race, was the 'I' born. That is when man said 'I' to himself for the first time. In the myth, this I-consciousness is depicted as a dwarf, as Alberich; it was felt to be something rising up from Nifelheim. Atlantis was Nifelheim, and it could justifiably be called the 'land of mists' (*Nebelheim*). Our earth atmosphere had not yet been cleared of its water vapours; there was as yet no precipitation in the form of rain. The human 'I' was born out of this Nifelheim with its seething waters and hanging mists. Wagner expresses this magnificently in the orchestra's E-flat major chord; the basic motif of our present humanity resounds out of Nifelheim.

Let us be clear what was happening on the Earth at that time. Man came to the Earth as a soul being. His body was born out of the ether-earth. [At that stage] man is still neither man nor woman, still knows nothing of possessions or property, nothing of power.

The soul is symbolized as water. Property, which is also power, is still guarded by the surging powers of the astral world, the Rhine maidens. But something is in slow preparation which emerges in the Atlantean period: the 'I', egotism. But this original soul-being contained something that man must now forgo: love that does not yet seek an external being but rests in itself. Alberich has to renounce this love that rests in itself. He can do this through the ring that binds everything of a human quality. As long as hermaphroditism was maintained, man did not need the ring. Only when he renounced soul love—hermaphroditism—did the ring have externally to join what was separated. Man now had to attain love in the union with another separate being. The ring is the symbol of the merging of separate individuals, the union of both sexes in the physical. When Alberich seizes the ring, he has to renounce love. Now comes the time when the human being can no longer create singly. Previously, body, soul, and spirit had been one. Now the godhead creates the body from outside. The sexes are antagonistic towards one another; they are depicted by the two giants Fafner and Fasolt. The human body has become unisexual.

In the old religions the human body is portrayed as a temple; the godhead works creatively on it from without. Since he has become an 'I', man has to create the inner temple, our soul, himself. Love is still contained in the creative godhead; it still works creatively on the 'outer temple'. In the myth this is where Wotan wants to take the ring from the giants,[65] but Erda appears and dissuades him from doing so. Erda is humanity's collective clairvoyant consciousness. The god should not keep the ring, which holds together what must dissolve in order to re-unite at a higher level later on when the sexes have neutralized one another once more. Thus, through the prophetic clairvoyant power of the earth consciousness, Wotan is prevented from getting the ring into his power; the ring stays with the giants. From now on there is only one sex in each person. Giants signify physical corporeality. Only now do the giants build Valhalla. In a fight over the ring, Fasolt is killed by Fafner; this is the dichotomy between the masculine and the feminine. One of the sexes is killed in every individual—a man kills the woman in himself, a woman [kills] the man [in herself].

But now higher consciousness must first be born out of the encompassing earthly consciousness. This happens through the union of Wotan with Erda, the issue of which is Brunhilde. There is still something in Brunhilde of the divine all-wisdom of cosmic consciousness. But initially this consciousness withdraws. By contrast, Wotan begets Siegmund and Sieglinde with an earthly woman. This is the hermaphroditism of the soul, the masculine-and-feminine soul. Neither can live on without the other. The feminine soul, Sieglinde, falls prey to Hunding; the soul has to yield to the physical brain. Now Siegmund's wanderings begin, the soul enclosed in the body. The soul is not strong enough to approach the divine, which is lost. The gods cannot protect Siegmund; his sword shatters on Wotan's spear.

Wotan has to resign his rulership to the human self operating completely in the sensory element, to Hagen the son of Alberich, to the principle of the lower self. All the powers swear an oath against the alliance of the masculine soul element with the feminine element. Wotan himself must stand by Fricka. Fricka represents the masculine-feminine soul at a higher level; she urges Wotan to dissolve the connection between the masculine and feminine soul at the earthly level. In life the masculine and feminine stay joined; but on Earth, blood, sensuality, is involved. This is profoundly indicated in the trait of incest. This is a prohibited element that plays into the situation and, if it remains dominant, Siegmund and Sieglinde, the physical aspect, must perish. Sieglinde is supposed to be destroyed by Brunhilde, all-encompassing consciousness. But Brunhilde supports her and gives her the horse Grane, which carries human beings through events on Earth. Brunhilde retreats into exile; a ring of fire surrounds her rock. Now clairvoyant consciousness is encircled by a fire that man, if he wishes to reach the all-encompassing consciousness once more, must pass through to be purified.

But Sieglinde, the soul-feminine aspect, gives birth to Siegfried, human consciousness, which is meant to ascend again to the heights. He grows up in seclusion with Mime. He must overcome the dragon, his lower nature, in order to obtain power. He also overcomes Mime.

Who is Mime? Mime is able to confer something that makes you invisible, the helmet of invisibility (*Tarnkappe*), something of a power that is not visible to ordinary people. The helmet of invisibility is the symbol of a magician—of both a white or a black magician—who walks visibly among us but is invisible as a magician. Mime is the magician who, using dark earthly forces, can bestow the *Tarnkappe*. He wants to turn Siegfried into a black magician, but Siegfried resists this. Siegfried kills the dragon, tastes a drop of its blood—symbol of the passions—and is thereby able to understand the language of the birds, of the sensory-earthly element. He can take the path of the higher initiate; he is shown the way to Brunhilde, to all-consciousness.

Up to now we have three phases of northern development: first the dwarf, then the giants, and now man. The *Valkyries* signify the second phase. And only in *Siegfried* do we have the birth of man himself. Enclosed in his bodily nature, he must find the way back to pure wisdom. The fourth part, *The Twilight of the Gods*, indicates that in the northern world man was not yet mature, that he had not yet reached a complete initiation. Siegfried is still vulnerable on a single spot—on the place where Christ carried the cross. Siegfried was not yet able to take on the cross. This is a profound expression for the fact that the northern peoples were still lacking something, that this Christianity was still a necessity for them. Siegfried is not able to unite with Brunhilde; he is the human soul, born of an earthly woman, of the union of Siegmund and Sieglinde. Brunhilde is what has remained virginal: higher consciousness.

In the last phase, higher knowledge must be attained. Because man has not yet attained the capacity to unite with virginal wisdom, he carries the aspiration for higher knowledge as a longing. This [lack of capacity] has to be overcome. And his earthly lust to unite with Brunhilde leads to an exchange of goods—she gives the horse, he the ring.

Until man is able to unite with his higher self, the ring, external coercion, retains its power. Man submerses himself in lower consciousness, he is afflicted with blindness. Siegfried forgets Brunhilde, he comes together with Gudrun, lower consciousness. He will even woo Brunhilde on Gunther's behalf, who is unworthy of her. This means that, in the last phase, before the coming of Christianity, man succumbs once more to the impure path, to dark forces. The wrongful alliance between Brunhilde and Gunther is the cause of Siegfried's downfall. He is forced to find death through the lower forces in whose power he has entangled himself.

The last phase draws near. The three Norns appear once more. It is the phase where all-encompassing consciousness is lost:

> The end, eternal knowledge![66]
> The wise say nothing more
> To the world: —
> Down to the Mother, down!

Higher wisdom, which previously had been given to the sons of the gods, is lost on Earth; it returns to the eternal. Humanity must now rely on itself.

The music drama *Tristan and Isolde* is, for someone who looks more deeply—and particularly so for Wagner,—a growing clarification of the problem of the twofold nature of sexuality. Male and female only have significance for the physical plane. There is a longing in Tristan to be separate no longer, to find the balance, to have a consciousness that is no longer masculine or feminine. This longing suffuses and weaves throughout the drama: to no longer be I-Tristan, but to have Isolde absorbed into oneself; to no longer be I-Isolde, but to be Isolde *and* Tristan. They both lose consciousness of this separation. Thus in the final words of this work there sounds out the redemption from separate existence:

> In the swelling tides[67]
> of the sea of bliss,
> in the resounding echoes
> of fragrant waves,
> in the drifting All
> of world-breath—
> to drown,
> to founder,
> unconscious—
> utmost rapture!

Every word is chosen out of a deeper knowledge. This swelling sea of bliss is the astral world, Devachan is the world sounding in fragrant tones. The world-breath is the life principle in which everything must be balanced out. No longer separated in consciousness, to drown in what is undifferentiated, to founder, unconscious—this is the utmost rapture. Indeed, it is utmost rapture for our earthly aspect to overcome sensuality out of the spirit. The rapture that strives for the annihilation of the earthly element has an ennobling quality; it is the overcoming of what it has in itself. This is the problem that Wagner tried to solve in *Tristan and Isolde.*

All these thoughts were not living in Wagner in a conscious, abstract way, but they lived in the myths and Wagner drew them from the myths. It is not necessary for the individual artist to have these as abstract thoughts in himself. Just as a plant grows according to laws without being aware of them, so cosmic forces live in myth as symbolic images of eternal, divine truth.

Wagner's Siegfried is still entangled in what is earthly; he has to perish in it. Brunhilde is aware of the greater picture, and understands what is involved. She surrenders the ring to the Rhine maidens, to the element that has not penetrated into the play of this world. The whole development of humanity goes back to original, virginal substance.

A new worldview takes the place of the old Nordic one, a worldview that no longer calls on what is external and sensual, but only on what has remained virginal, on the soul. Brunhilde, who is still entangled in the external sensual element through her union with Siegfried, rides into the fire. From this, love is born. This is a thought that is initially still tragic for the North, for what people were able to understand is destroyed. From the sea of fire, from the original virginal substance, love is born out of the spirit. *Et incarnatus est de Spiritu Sancto ex Maria virgine.*[68] Out of the same element from which previously egotism, sensual love, was born, a new feeling is now born that is exalted above everything entangled in the physical plane. Wisdom retreats so that out of a portion of the element that has preserved maidenly purity, love can arise. This is Christ, the Christian principle. Selfless love in contrast to selfish love—this is the great evolution that is purchased by the mysterious involution of death, the demise of the physical. We have kept a strict contrast between life and death.

Wood is dried-up life, and on this wood hangs the new, eternal Life from which the new era is now born. A new, spiritual life emerges from the Twilight of the Gods. Wagner longed to depict this Christian principle in its depths and, after he had gone through the four phases of Nordic life, he did so in his *Parsifal.* This is the fifth phase. Because Wagner had experienced the tragic element in northern development, he felt a need for the glorification of Christianity.

Lecture 4

BERLIN, 19 MAY 1905

THE deeper we penetrate into Richard Wagner's work, the deeper we enter into theosophical and mystical questions and enigmas of life. It is of exceptional significance that, having worked on the whole prehistory of the European peoples in four stages in his *Ring of the Nibelung*, Wagner then created an eminently Christian drama, the work with which he actually completed his life, his *Parsifal*.[69] We need to penetrate Wagner's whole personality if we want to understand what is really contained in this *Parsifal*.

Ever since the 40s he had had the idea of working on the figure of Jesus of Nazareth. He wanted—and fragments of this still exist—to write a drama called *Jesus of Nazareth*,[70] a work in which infinite love, in the way it took effect in Jesus of Nazareth for the whole of humanity, would be depicted. He wanted to create this but couldn't get beyond the basic idea. In the 50s he sketched out his drama *Die Sieger* (The Victors). In these dramas we can see from what depths of his worldview Wagner drew his intuitions.

Let's look briefly at the content of the drama *Die Sieger*. Ananda, a youth of high caste, is loved passionately by Prakriti, a chandala girl, a girl from a despised caste. But he renounces all earthly, sensual love and becomes a disciple of Buddha. The way Wagner envisioned it, the chandala girl had been a member of the Brahmin caste in a previous incarnation, who at that time had spurned with haughty contempt the love of a chandala youth. Her karmic punishment now was to be reborn into the chandala caste. Once she has worked on herself to the point where she can forgo her love, she also becomes a disciple of Buddha. You can see that Wagner had already apprehended the problem of karma in all its depths when in the 50s he set about creating such a profoundly serious music drama as *Die Sieger*. All these thoughts finally came together in his *Parsifal*. But at the centre of *Parsifal* there is also the question of Christ.

There is an important moment in the history of the Middle Ages at the turn of the twelfth and thirteenth centuries. Wolfram von Eschenbach was active at this time, who, out of the deepest spirituality of the Middle Ages, worked the mystery of Parzival into a literary form. There was something living in those who had a spiritual life during the Middle Ages, which in initiated circles was called an elevation [or intensification] of love. The minstrels of courtly love, minnesingers, had existed before this time and continued to do so afterwards, but there was a great difference between what had previously been regarded as sensual, worldly love, and what arose later in Christianity as refined, purified love. An important monument to this turning point in medieval spiritual life is preserved for us in Hartmann von Aue's *Der arme Heinrich* (Poor Henry).[71] This deeply spiritual work is permeated by the spiritual teaching the knights of the Crusades had brought back with them from the East.

Let's recall the content of *Der arme Heinrich*: A Swabian knight for whom up to now everything had gone well, is stricken by an incurable disease, by leprosy, and can only be cured by the sacrificial death of a pure virgin. A virgin is found who is prepared to sacrifice herself for him. They go together to a famous doctor in Salerno in Italy. The maiden is about to be sacrificed, but at the last moment Heinrich refuses to let the sacrifice proceed. The maiden's life is spared, Heinrich becomes well again, and they marry.

Here again we find the image of a pure virgin who sacrifices herself for someone who had previously lived only in sensuality and is now saved by her. From the viewpoint of the Middle Ages, there is a mystery hidden here. Minnesinging was ascribed to an ancient stream that had come up through the four successive stages of European cultural development, just as we find them depicted in the legends of Richard Wagner's tetralogy. Love arising from sensuality was regarded with hindsight in that period as something that should be overcome. Minnesinging was to arise in a new form through the higher spiritual power of Christianity.

If we want to understand what was happening here, we have to draw all the factors together in order to recall the character, the physiognomy, of those times; then we can understand what motivated Wagner to portray these legends. There was an ancient legend, a primordial legend, that we can find in the oldest Germanic peoples and in a somewhat different form in Italy and other lands as well. Let's look at the basic outline of this legend: A man who has known all the pleasures of the world makes his way now into a kind of subterranean cave. There he meets a woman of ultra-attractive appealing power. He experiences certain pleasures of Paradise there; but then he is overcome by a longing for the upper world, and after some time returns from the mountain. This is particularly clearly portrayed in the Tannhäuser legend. When we consider this legend, we have in it a beautiful symbol for the aspiration of love in the Germanic lands before the great turning-point I mentioned: Man's activity in the sensual world, the withdrawal to the pleasures of love in the ancient sense, which one saw embodied in the goddess Venus, and experiencing the distraction from activities in the outer world through love as a kind of paradisal experience. But in this form the legend has no real centre. It has nothing that gives us a view to what is higher. Thus it has arisen from the previous view, from the preceding form of love. Later, in the beginnings of the development of love in spiritual form through Christianity, people wanted to highlight the earlier period and show the contrast between Paradise then and the idea of Paradise in Christianity.

If we want to understand Wagner, we need to go even deeper. We have looked at our fifth root-race. After floods had covered Atlantis, the [post-Atlantean] sub-races emerged: the ancient Indian, the ancient Persian, then the Egyptian-Babylonian-Assyrian-Chaldean, then the Greco-Latin, and after the decline of Roman civilization our fifth sub-race arises in which we are living today and has significance particularly for Christian Europe. It was not that Richard Wagner was consciously aware of everything I have just mentioned; but he had an absolutely certain feeling for the situation of the fifth sub-race in the world, and experienced the whole task of the present as a religious one, in a way that even in theosophy couldn't be better formulated.

You know that each 'race' was inspired by great initiates, and that the original inspiration for the fifth Atlantean sub-race proceeded from the so-called Proto-Semites. You know that as Atlantis was swallowed by floods, those who migrated away and were preserved from the destruction of the race, were led by a manu, by a divine guide, to the Gobi Desert in Asia. Waves of civilization went out from there, initially via India to the Middle East, Persia, Assyria, to Egypt, and then to Southern Europe, to Greece, Rome, and later into our regions.

The first two waves of Semitic civilization are historically untraceable; they are the impulses preserved by the Indian and ancient Persian race. But when we look at the Chaldean-Egyptian sub-race, we have to say that a great Semitic impulse took place there, from which the people of Israel derive their name. Christianity can be traced back to a Semitic wave of this kind, which then extended into the civilization of Greece and Rome. If we follow this cultural wave still further, we find the Semitic influence spreading through all of Europe through the Moorish peoples who invaded Spain, which even the Christian monks could not evade. In this way the primordial Semitic impulse reaches into the fifth root-race. We see that in this one great stream primal culture is influenced five times.

We have a great spiritual stream growing from the south towards another stream that has developed in the north through four stages of primal culture, until the two streams flow together. At the turn of the twelfth and thirteenth centuries, a worldly and naive people is influenced by the culture coming up from the south. The incursion of a new culture was experienced like a spiritual stream of fresh air. Wolfram von Eschenbach was entirely within the influence of this spiritual steam.

The northern culture is symbolized in the legend of Tannhäuser, where the impulse also comes from the south. Everywhere we find something we can define as the Semitic impulse. But there was something that people felt very powerfully: that the Germanic race was the last limb of an evolutionary process, that something completely new had to come, that something completely different was in preparation for the fifth root-race—namely, the high mission of Christianity.

There was a longing in the Germanic lands at that time for a new form of Christianity. A new Christianity had to be created; it had to be released from what it had undergone in the south. Christianity had to be re-created in a purer form. During the period of the Crusades a dichotomy emerged between Rome and Jerusalem. The Crusaders fought with the battle cries of 'for Rome!' and 'for Jerusalem!' The one was referring to Roman Christianity, now just a shell, and the other referred to a pure Christianity people wished to re-establish, for which Jerusalem was seen as a spiritual centre. This is what the scholastics thought, and so also for Dante in his *Divine Comedy*,[72] Jerusalem was a centre which was to be sought—but more in a spiritual than in an external sense. Thus the fifth sub-race was felt to be a harbinger of the future. The old influences had ceased; something completely new had to come; a new vortex of world civilization began. It was only an attempt at establishing a proper Christianity, but a kernel of genuine Christianity was to be peeled out of this shell. At the turn of the Middle Ages people sensed a decline, the end of something they had experienced as a blessing, and at the same time they felt something on the rise in their longing for the new. All this was living in Wolfram von Eschenbach.

Now look at our new times. Imagine this feeling renewed in a time when the decline had arrived, and you will find something of what Richard Wagner was experiencing. Much of what was felt earlier as a decline of the race had in the meantime come to pass. From the beginning of his conscious life, Wagner had felt this declining element particularly vividly. For him there were many symptoms indicating that the decline had come and that a new structuring had to take place. No one felt more deeply than Wagner the chaos that surrounds us today in many respects: the way the lower classes in our time waste away rather than live to the full, the misery of the great mass of European peoples whose mental and spiritual life remains in darkness, who are excluded from all higher education. And because of this, in 1848 Wagner became a revolutionary. We mustn't imagine Wagner as a regular revolutionary, but we need to picture him as having a thought that weighed heavily on his soul: [the thought that] it is in our hands whether we take part, whether we accelerate the decline, turn the wheel downwards, or lead it upwards. For him the revolution of 1848 was only an external opportunity.

When we look at all this in this way, we will understand how Richard Wagner came to his ideas on the races, how he expressed this in his prose writing. In his work *Religion und Kunst* (Religion and Art)[73] he says roughly the following: Over in Asia, in the Indian nation, we have something of the original energy of the Aryan race. An element is living there of an elevated spiritual life, but only for an elite, for Brahmins. The lower castes are excluded from these teachings, but a high spiritual standpoint is achieved in the Brahmin, which is an expression of the primordial culture. If from there we look to the north, so Wagner said, we have there a naive race that has itself passed through four stages of development, a people who love hunting, of whom we must imagine that, as hunters, they have pleasure in killing their enemies. Pleasure in killing[74] is for Wagner a symptom of decadence. It is a profound occult fact that life and death are connected in a remarkable way with the development of the individual towards what is higher, purer, spiritual. Everything a person does by way of causing suffering, of destroying life, drains his soul of spiritual power. No matter what one might think of certain cultural phenomena, any destruction of life is connected with a stripping away of spiritual forces. This is why one who follows the 'dark path' has to destroy life. This is expressed, for example, in the novel by Mabel Collins, *The Blossom and the Fruit.*[75] It is the story of a female black magician who destroys unborn life because she needs it for her reprehensible powers. There is a deep connection between life, death, and man's development. This is a lesson that has to be learnt and gone through by different peoples. Things were slightly different in a particular period of development when people killed in a naive way; at that time people experienced the energy in themselves when they killed. This was the situation with the old Germanic hunter tribes.

Now, with the coming of Christianity, this has changed. Christian teaching has a prohibition against killing; killing is a sin. Here we find the origin of a view that led Wagner to be a strict vegetarian. For him, eating meat was a sign of the decline of a race, and saw an ascent only being possible when people adopt a form of nourishment that no longer involves killing.

The sense that a new impulse had to come also led Wagner to his remarks on the influence of Judaism in modern culture. Wagner was not anti-Semitic in an irrational, hateful sense that one might experience him as being today, but felt that Judaism as such had played its part, that the Semitic influences on our culture had to fade away and something new had to take their place. Hence his call for a renewal. This is connected with how he saw our present race. He said to himself: We must make a distinction between development of the race and development of the soul. We have to make this distinction if we are to have any understanding at all of development.

We were all once incarnated in the Atlantean race. But while souls have evolved further and climbed higher, the race has fallen into decadence. But every ascent is associated with a decline. For every individual who ennobles and purifies themself, there is someone who sinks lower. There is a difference between the soul in the racial body and the racial body itself. The more man becomes like the race—the more he loves what is temporal, transient, tied to the attributes of the race—the more he belongs to the downfall of the race. The more he frees himself, lifts himself out of racial characteristics, the more the soul has the possibility of incarnating at a higher level. A spirit like Wagner, who distinguishes between evolution of the soul and evolution of the race, simply cannot be anti-Semitic. He knows that it is not souls that have finished their role, but the races that have played out and completed their tasks in the greater picture of world development. This is always what Wagner is expressing when he speaks of 'Semitism'. Wagner feels the downfall, the decline of the races, and the necessity of the ascent of souls. This necessity was also felt by medieval souls like Wolfram von Eschenbach or Hartmann von Aue.

Let's go back to the legend of poor Henry. We need to look more deeply into what it means that poor Henry was healed by a pure maiden. Henry is sick because initially he has been living in sensuality; his 'I' is born out of his race, out of what, during that era, worked on the senses. This 'I', born out of the element active on the senses, becomes sick as the call goes out to humanity to develop itself to a higher stage. His soul becomes sick because it connects itself with what should only live in the race. This is characterized by love coming to expression in a worldly way. But now a higher love should be developed out of the lower love that lives in the race. What is living in the race must be redeemed by something higher, by a higher, pure love that sacrifices itself for the aspiring human soul, by what Goethe calls the Eternal Feminine, which draws us on.

You know—I have often spoken about it—that the masculine and feminine are living in every human being, and that because they are separated out, the sensual element intrudes. Redemption by the 'Eternal Feminine' means that the sensual element is overcome. This is also depicted in *Tristan and Isolde.* For both Wolfram von Eschenbach and Richard Wagner the historical expression for this overcoming is Parsifal. He is the representative of the new Christianity. Parsifal becomes king of the Holy Grail because he liberates what had previously suffered under the servitude of the senses, and brings a new principle of love into the world.

What is the basis of *Parsifal*? What is the significance of the Grail? The original legend which emerges around the middle of the Middle Ages tells us that the Grail is the cup Christ used at the Last Supper and in which Joseph of Arimathea collected the blood that flowed from the wounds of Christ Jesus. This cup, and the spear that made the wounds, were lifted up by angels and preserved hovering in the air until Titurel built a castle on the mountain of Montsalvat—that is, the mountain of healing—in which the cup was preserved as a sanctuary of spiritual knighthood. Twelve knights are gathered there to serve the Grail. It has the power to divert death from these knights, and to give them what they need to turn their souls to the spiritual. The sight of it always gives them renewed spiritual strength.

Now, to start with, we can look at the form Richard Wagner gave the Parsifal saga. In essence it is the same as the one we have from Wolfram von Eschenbach. On the one hand we have the Grail temple with its knights, and on the other we have the magic castle of Klingsor with its knights, who are the real enemies of the Grail knights. Two kinds of Christianity are contrasted with each other: the one representing the knights of the Grail, and the other, Klingsor with his knights. Klingsor is the one who has mutilated himself so as not to fall into sensuality. But he has not overcome the craving for it; he has only made it impossible to satisfy the craving. Hence he still lives in the realm of sensuality. He is served by enchanted maidens. Kundry is the actual temptress in this realm. She draws towards the sensual side everything that comes to Klingsor, in a way belonging to the past. Klingsor is a personification of medieval Christianity, which has become ascetic, has mortified sensuality but not desire. It does not save one from the seductive force of sensual love which is personified in Kundry. Something higher was seen in a higher spirituality's power of renunciation, which does not deaden sensuality by coercion but purifies it through higher spiritual knowledge and raises itself up into the realm of purified love. Amfortas and the Grail knights aspire to this, but up to now it has not been possible to reach this realm. Their efforts failed. As long as the proper spiritual power was absent, Amfortas had to fall to the temptation of Kundry. The higher disposition in Amfortas falls victim to the lower disposition in Klingsor.

Thus the Parsifal saga depicts two phenomena side by side. On the one side is Christianity become ascetic but nevertheless unable to attain higher spiritual knowledge by deadening sensuality. On the other side are the representatives of spiritual knighthood which, however, will always fall victim to Klingsor's temptations until the redeemer appears who will conquer Klingsor. Amfortas is wounded, loses the spear to Klingsor, and must guard the Grail as a king racked with pain. Thus higher Christianity is ailing and suffers. In suffering it must guard the real secrets, the mysteries of Christianity connected with the Grail, until a redeemer in a new form appears—and this redeemer arises in Parsifal. Parsifal must first learn his lessons, undergo tests; he then purifies himself and rises to the spiritual force, to the feeling, of the great unity of all being. Wagner depicts profound occult truths in Parsifal, but, again, unconsciously. The first stage Parsifal passes through is where he learns compassion, compassion for our older brothers, the animals. In an impetuous urge to become a knight, he leaves his mother Herzeleide, who dies of grief.

Parsifal then fights, and kills an animal [a swan]. At the sight of the dying animal he experiences what it means to kill. This is the first stage of his purification.

At the second stage he learns to overcome desire without having to mortify the external organs of sensual desire. He comes to the Grail the first time but does not yet recognize his task. He learns to know it through the initiation of life. He appears to fall to Kundry's temptations, but passes the trial. At the moment when he might have succumbed to the temptation, he wrests from himself the power of desire. A new, a pure love shines in him like a rising sun. There flashes up what we saw arising in the Twilight of the Gods. '*Et incarnatus est de Spiritu Sancto ex Maria virgine*,' born of the spirit through the virgin—this is the higher power of love, which is born in the soul that is not pervaded by sensuality, and which cleanses, purifies, refines all souls. Human beings must awaken a soul like this in themselves, which does not mortify the sensual organs but refines all sensuality, because the I, the Christ, is born out of virginal matter. Christ is born in Parsifal. A higher, virginal power opposes seductive Kundry. Kundry, that feminine element which pulls the human Ego down into the sphere of sexuality, has to be overcome. In Kundry we meet the incarnation of that which, as the opposite sex, has pulled the human being down. Kundry has existed before—as Herodias who demands the head of John the Baptist. She existed in a way similar to Ahasver, as a figure who can find no rest, who looks everywhere for her sole salvation in sensual love.

What Wagner has unconsciously hidden for us in his *Parsifal* is liberation from sensual love. We see how this thought twines its way up in his work. By the intuitive force of his being, already in *The Flying Dutchman* he is led to the same problem: a man who wanders the seas, is freed from his long wanderings by the sacrifice of a virgin. It is also the problem in *Tannhäuser*. Wagner depicts the minstrels' contest at Wartburg as a battle between the minstrel of the old, sensual love—Heinrich von Ofterdingen—and Wolfram von Eschenbach who represents the power of renewed, spiritual Christianity. In the legend of this singing contest at Wartburg it is precisely Heinrich von Ofterdingen who calls upon the help of Master Klingsor from

Ungarland. But they are both conquered by the force that flows from Wolfram von Eschenbach. We now get a deeper understanding of Tristan, because we know that it is not about the mortification of love but of the purification and catharsis of the love that is alive in him.

From Schopenhauer's[76] negation of the will, Richard Wagner lifts himself up to a return and purification of the will in the higher spheres. Wagner even brought this to expression in a drama that doesn't appear to contain it at all—in the *Meistersingers*. It is there between the lines, as it were, in the purification of Hans Sachs from the temptation he feels to win Eva for himself. This is not so much in the text as in the music; when you hear the music of the *Meistersingers* you sense something of this purification.

All this came together for Wagner in his *Parsifal.* He had looked back to the original Brahmanic ideal. He saw with sorrow and pain the symptoms of decline in the present race. And he wanted to create a new impulse out of his art. The redemption of the race through a new spiritual content—this is what he wanted to give in his festival plays. Before he parted ways with Wagner, Nietzsche[77] also wrote in this spirit about Dionysian art. He felt that something of a renewal of the mystery plays of Ancient Greece was living in the festival plays. The 'Dionysias' of Aeschylus and Sophocles,[78] who take us back to the beginning of the fourth sub-race, were something that had contributed to the ascent of the cultural stream of the fifth sub-race. This redemption was experienced in the depths of the mystery temple of Dionysus. What had taken place in those times in the mystery temples came out first in European lands. We stand before a Dionysus who incarnates into matter, celebrates his resurrection in the human being, and his ascension into heaven. In the mystery temples, the Greek initiate experienced the descended god. There was something of a mood of sorrow in these Greek mysteries when it was said that in the future the god would rise again in human hearts. And in the northern sagas, the initiate Druids spoke of a Twilight of the Gods from which a new generation would arise. [The coming of] Christianity was prophezied in the ancient mysteries of the Druids. Richard Wagner saw the time being close at hand when Christianity must come to fulfilment, which had emerged in its first stages in the fourth, and had to evolve further in the fifth sub-race, in which this Christianity will speak its own unique language. Those who had been believers should now become 'beholders'.

Richard Wagner felt the pulse of earthly development, just as Édouard Schuré [79] did, who, working out of this impulse, reconstructed the ancient mystery drama of the Eleusinian Mysteries. Thus the event at Bayreuth shows us the coming together of two cultural streams: a revival of the mysteries of Greece, and a new Christianity. Thus Wagner, those around him, and also Édouard Schuré, felt this art to be the first prelude to a reunification of what had once split apart. In the original drama [at Eleusis], religion, art, and science were united as one until they separated. Art began to exist on its own—Aeschylus, Sophocles—and religion and science went their own ways. Three streams, running alongside each other, thus grew from their common root in the Greek mysteries. Initially each of these streams could only become great by going its own way. Time found a specific religious expression for the heart, an artistic one for the senses, and a scientific expression for the rational mind. This had to happen, for only when people were able to unfold these capacities to their highest blossoming, but on separate paths, could a perfection be attained. Religion taken to the height of the Christian worldview is willing to unite again with art and science. Poetry, painting, sculptural art, and music will only reach their zenith when they unite once more with genuine religion. And science, which has only come to full development in modern times, has in truth given the impulse for the unification of these three streams.

Now, through Wagner—who was one of the first to sense the impulse for a new union of art, science, and religion—this reuniting is offered to humanity as a new gift of consecration. He felt that Christianity is called upon to reunite what was previously separated, and incorporated this into his figure of Parsifal. That magical quality of Good Friday, which Wagner has set into his Good Friday mood, rings in our ears like the great sounding of a new culture. He recognized that soul development and race development must take separate paths, that it is important to lift souls and redeem them, that the resurrection of souls must be brought to pass despite the tragic destiny of being bound up with the body of the race which is in decline. Wagner wanted his works in Bayreuth to sound out the world of tone that points to a new future. A small part of humanity at least should hear those musical tones of the future. What Wagner made known to his time is a living, artistic apocalypse; [he did this] like a true prophet who wants to point to a new era he knows will soon dawn. His life's work fades away like this: I will make known to you the faces that have appeared to me, and the time will come in which they will be realized.

Lecture 5

COLOGNE, 3 DECEMBER 1905

Parzival and Lohengrin

WE want to look today at the world of medieval legends from the perspective of the theosophical worldview. There are two important legends that are characteristic of the intellectual and spiritual development of Europe in the Middle Ages: the two legends connected with the Grail.

Concerning the deepest truths, the sages of earlier times spoke to the people through myths and legends. If, in those times, one had tried to teach the people living in the regions of Northern and Central Europe the sort of concepts we hear today in the theosophical worldview, the people of that period would have got nothing from it. The sages spoke to every nation and era in a way that nation and era could understand. In doing so, they always took into account the law of rebirth or reincarnation.

The sages who told the peoples of Northern and Central Europe the secrets of the world, were Druids. *Druid* means 'oak'. When it is said that the Teutons worshipped 'under oak trees', this did not only mean that they worshipped under actual oaks, but also that they were led by Druids. And when it is said that Boniface 'cut down the oak tree', this signifies that the old Druid religion was conquered by Christendom.[80] A real truth is related here in legend form; the Druids wove real truths into their legends. All the souls who take up our worldview today were once addressed by a Druid priest. He spoke to them in a way that was suited to those times. All of us who absorb the theosophical worldview have heard the same things before in myths and legends, otherwise we should not understand them at all.

This is the secret of the great Masters: they live in the consciousness that they are among people who incarnate again and again.

Throughout the Middle Ages the fundamental truths of Germanic Central European culture lived in a great legend. When we get acquainted with this legend, we understand the nature of the Middle Ages. The Druid priests cultivated an awareness that, far in the West, there had once been an advanced civilization. This civilization had been in a land called Nifelheim or Nibelungenheim. This Nifelheim was Ancient Atlantis. It had once been a 'Nebelheim', a place of mists [Ger. *Nebel* = mist] because of its peculiar atmospheric conditions which were completely different from our own.

This primordial Germanic legend is thus really relating the truth. It points to an ancient primal land that once existed between Europe and America, where the Atlantic Ocean now is. This very ancient land of Atlantis sank, and with it went treasures of power and wisdom. These treasures are referred to as gold, and their demise is related in the legend as the sinking of the Nibelung's horde of gold. The Nibelung treasure has to be raised up in a new way, awoken, and further towards the East, in Europe. First Wotan and then Siegfried were the initiates whose task it was to bring back to present-day Europe the ancient treasure, to make fruitful once more, in a certain way, the Nibelung horde for the newer civilization. The fact that the legend presents us with an initiate 'Wotan', helps us to look deeply into another very ancient civilization. The letters W and B correspond to each other. Wotan, Woden is the same as Bodha, Buddha. Wotan is indeed the Germanic form of the word Buddha. This brings us to a common origin of the European Wotan religion and the Asiatic Buddha religion. The Buddha religion did not spread so much in India as among the peoples of Asia who still had something of the Atlantean culture in them. The Wotan peoples had also brought their way of seeing things from Atlantean culture. Their further development was expressed in the legends told to them by their Druid priests. The rescuing of the Nibelung treasure—Atlantean culture—is expressed particularly beautifully in Wotan and Siegfried.

In these legends, which can be found from Russia to France and England via Germany, there is a tragic prophetic quality which can be seen everywhere where Druids taught. This prophecy said: A Twilight of the Gods will come. We are what remains of Atlantean civilization. We have to die out so that something better can enter. Our initiates are prophets of what is coming. In all those who are initiated in the same way as Siegfried, a definite quality of tragedy comes to expression. 'The Song of the Nibelungs' contains a very ancient form of initiation: the Nibelungs' distress, the Nibelungs' lament. The very advanced pupils were taught that another would come who would bring spiritual life. The mood of the Twilight of the Gods spread everywhere. All lived with a sense—and the advanced pupils with the certainty—that another would come who would be completely different from their initiates. This was expressed in the legend of Siegfried.

In Scandinavia and Russia they had the *Drotte* mysteries which corresponded to the Druid mysteries. *Drotte* is another term for Druid. Everywhere in the old mysteries the name of the original great initiate is Sig. All names that contain 'Sig-' can be traced back to Sig, like Sigurd, Sigmund, Sieglinde and so on, for example. Siegfried was the initiate who had found peace in initiation. '*Friede*' [Ger. = peace] means that which leads people beyond all doubt; it is the satisfaction of a longing, the longing for knowledge, for power. In all the portrayals of him, Siegfried is depicted as being invulnerable. The Greek initiate Achilles, was vulnerable on one spot, on his heel. After slaying the dragon, Siegfried becomes invulnerable except for a spot between his shoulder blades. That is where the cross is to be borne. This symbol played a profound role in the ancient mysteries. They said there: You are all vulnerable on the place where One will have to carry the cross. The One who covers over this place with the cross, the cross-bearer, will be the great initiate who is no longer vulnerable. This gives the Nordic legend its great quality. This wisdom was an apocalyptic wisdom.

All occultists know that this wisdom spreads out from a central oracle-site of twelve initiates, from the so-called White Lodge. Wisdom is carried out from there into the world. And never is the situation other than that each individual is aware of his connection with the others. Everywhere there were twelve members of the Lodge.

Such too were the Apostles. The consciousness of those who only had intimations, and the wisdom of those who really knew, led back to the Round Table of King Arthur. This is no less than the great White Lodge which, in the Siegfried initiation, related to the people what it had to say to the world. Great initiates were members of the Round Table, which existed up to the time of Queen Elizabeth I of England. Then it was closed down for political reasons.

Two very distinct political currents led the consciousness of ordinary people in the Middle Ages back to primal times. Among the Franks, who were fortunate enough to conquer the west of Europe, there was a ruling dynasty which actually traced its origin back to the time of Atlantis. They were called the Wibelungs or Nibelungs, from which the word Ghibelline[81] later arose. There was an old awareness of a ruling dynasty arising in the Franks that had its roots in the ancient Nibelung land and which combined in itself both worldly might and priestly power. This is why Charlemagne sought to be crowned in Rome, in order to add a spiritual element to the worldly one.

Originally, the assumption of power was derived from what had been brought over from Atlantis. Because it was thought and sensed that a Twilight of the Gods was coming, a certain tragic quality was connected with the ruling dynasty. It was said: Those who want to know can certainly become initiates, but they must be superseded by something else. This mood was initially expressed in the well-known legend of Barbarossa. Something was then added that is not included in the usual legend. Barbarossa was rightly seen as a continuation of the old Frankish rulers. The Hohenstaufen were the Ghibellines, Waiblings, Wibelungs, Nibelungs, in contrast to the Welfs, the Guelphs. The more penetrating tale adds to the well-known Barbarossa legend that Barbarossa brought the Holy Grail from Asia to Europe. As a physical personality, he himself lost his life in the process, and now waits for his time to come. In this is expressed the whole mood of the Middle Ages with regard to the old heathendom and the new Christendom.

People began to consider their own folk-soul and said: We brought our culture from old Atlantis. But it is destined to perish; Christianity must take its place. But it will rise again purified, cleansed, raised up by Christianity. People began to make a transition from the end of the decline to the beginning of the ascent. People began to regard the course of a deeper Germanic spiritual culture as one whereby the clairvoyant Atlantean consciousness was superseded by something still to come. One had once more to master natural boldness, piety, virtue, but in a new way. People had three notions, an idea of three definite forces: Wotan [Odin], Vili, and Vé.[82] Wotan is intuitive power as depicted by the initiate; Vili is the will itself; Vé is the heart *(Gemüt)* with a tragic quality, where it becomes apocalyptic. Now a new time was to come. Now, through Christian teaching, a transition was to be made, and one was to ascend again to what had been before the Twilight of the Gods.

That Barbarossa is waiting in a mountain indicates that he is an initiate. A 'mountain' is the place of initiation. Christ went with his disciples 'up into a mountain'—into mysterium. Ravens signify an initiation for Barbarossa. In the Persian initiation ritual a distinction was made between seven levels of initiation. 'Raven' means the first level of personal initiation. Ravens indicate the connection that still exists between the initiate and his surroundings. We can think of Elijah's ravens. We also find ravens in relation to Wotan; they transmit his communications to the surrounding world. Thus the initiate Barbarossa also had ravens around him, which maintained his connection with the world.

Barbarossa had brought the Holy Grail from the Orient. This Holy Grail was preserved on *Mons Salvationis*, the mountain of salvation. It is now surrounded by the successors of King Arthur's Round Table, the twelve knights who received Christian initiation in addition to the old pagan initiation. The Grail is the symbol of Christian initiation. One who wished to be initiated into the secrets of the Holy Grail became a Christian initiate. One became a Christian initiate by passing first through all forms of doubt, and then finding a firm footing in a connection with Christ himself. One thing is necessary for this: direct trust in the figure of Christ. The first disciples laid such particular emphasis on the fact that Christ had been *among* them. They said: We want to bear witness that we were with him. We touched his wounds with our hands. What we make known is what we have seen and heard ourselves. Paul became an Apostle because he truly saw the Risen One in spirit. What matters is the unmediated *experience,* attained not through wisdom and logic but *directly.*

It is clear to us what Parzival needs to achieve on his wanderings. Parzival's mother is called *Herzeleide* [Germ.: *Herz* = heart; *Leiden* = suffering]. Wolfram von Eschenbach was an initiate; if we read his *Parzival* with profound attention, between the lines and words, we find that the name Herzeleide, Parzival's mother, is precipitated from the tragic quality that lay in the German heart. One who does not take the Parzival path bears suffering in their heart; they have to struggle through to peace. Wolfram von Eschenbach knew how to clothe the legend in a wonderfully beautiful form. With this one fact [i.e. the name Herzeleide] he intended a deeply inward symbol (bearing in mind that a feminine individual always signifies consciousness): namely, that Herzeleide is the condition of consciousness with which Parzival sets out. Initially he has a tragic consciousness. He struggles his way, with a naive, simple consciousness, through everything that worldly knighthood can offer, in order to come to the secret of the Holy Grail.

We must hold this in conjunction with the Barbarossa legend. Barbarossa went to Asia to seek the secrets of the Holy Grail, Christian initiation. But he lost his life on the way to the Holy Grail. He has to wait 'in the mountain' until Christianity can connect with the former initiation. Barbarossa brought Christianity but did not achieve the deeper initiation of Christianity.

Parzival is the new Christian initiate, the great symbol that succeeds the Siegfried initiation. Siegfried conquered his lower nature, the dragon, the snake. Parzival becomes the initiate of the Holy Grail, who comes to know Him who is invulnerable where Siegfried was still vulnerable. The original idea of Christianity is brought to expression in Parzival. He no longer knows the idea of reincarnation. A single life between birth and death was seen as the only one. It was the one incarnation that had value. People no longer looked up to manas, buddhi, atma. Parzival-initiation was directed only towards reaching a consciousness of our connection with Christ, to considering only *one* incarnation in which the human being reaches knowledge through compassion, and not compassion through knowledge as happens in theosophy. Theosophy teaches us to recognize how we are connected with all human beings. Through it we realize that we are ourselves responsible for what our brother does. Theosophy leads to compassion through knowledge. But humanity had for a time to pass through a period of development where it was to find knowledge through compassion. It had to go down into the depths of compassion, because one can also reach knowledge there. It had to be like this so that people learnt to know the full importance of this earthly world. Christianity was to educate humanity so that the significance of the earthly would be understood. For this reason humanity had first, in a moral respect, to be conducted, led down, to physical life. Only then could it come to the great achievements that begin in urban culture.

The progress of the Middle Ages is portrayed in legend in the transition from the Parzival saga to the Lohengrin saga. This [Lohengrin] saga emerges in the period when towns were being founded all over Europe, which serve primarily the awakening middle classes and are based no longer on the spiritual life but on material life. All material achievements were promoted in the towns—like the art of printing for example, among other things. Without an urban culture, modern science would not have been able to develop in the way it has. The universities too are a consequence of this culture. Without it a Copernicus, a Kepler, Newton and so on would not have been possible. Even Dante's *Divine Comedy* and the painters of the Renaissance lead us back to urban culture.

The legend of the connection between Parzival, the father, and Lohengrin, the son, points to the significance of urban culture. Elsa von Brabant represents the towns, urban consciousness. In all mysticism, that which counteracts the physical world is portrayed as something feminine. Goethe speaks of the 'Eternal Feminine'; in Egypt this aspect was worshipped as Isis.

Let's keep in mind the chela's stages of initiation. To begin with, the chela has to overcome three stages.

The first stage is that of 'the Homeless One', where the person is torn away from the physical world, where he becomes objective towards the physical world. He has to unlearn partiality, he must learn to love everything equally; he does not love less but extends his love to everything that deserves love, not only to his homeland and so on.

The second stage is where the chela builds huts. He finds a new home. The disciples on the mountain have reached this stage. They are beyond space and time; they see Elias and Moses. This is why they say: Let us build tabernacles [huts].[83]

The third stage is that of the Swan. A Swan is a chela who has progressed so far that all things speak to him, including those that have their consciousness on higher planes. The animal's consciousness is on the astral plane, the plant's on the mental plane (rupa plane), the mineral's on the higher mental plane (arupa plane). One must lift oneself up to higher worlds in order to find the 'I', the name, of other beings; at that level they utter their own names to the chela. The world then sounds and rings out everywhere for him. With regard to this fact, Goethe says: [literal translation]

> The sun sounds out in ancient wise
> In contest of song in spheres of brotherhood,
> And completes its preordained journey
> With rolls of thunder.[84]

He repeats this indication from the 'Prologue in Heaven' at the point where Faust is taken up into higher worlds: [literal translation]

> The new day is born
> Sounding forth for spirit-ears.
> Rocky arches creak and rattle
> Phoebus' wheels roll and clatter,
> What a din comes with the light!
> There's drumming and trumpeting,
> The eye blinks, the ear is amazed,
> Nothing outrageous is heard.[85]

It is not a matter of indifference that [both] the 'Prologue in Heaven' in the first part of *Faust*, and the second part, begin in this way. Goethe is pointing here to something very specific: it is the third stage of chelaship where the world around us starts to sound and all things tell us their names. Jesus had reached this stage when he was to incorporate the Christ. In the White Lodge, this stage is called the Swan. Swans were those who were no longer permitted to say their own name, but to whom the whole world revealed its names.

Lohengrin, the son of Parzival, is the initiate who founded urban culture, who was sent out by the great Grail Lodge to fructify the consciousness of medieval humanity. Elsa von Brabant is a depiction of aspiring human consciousness which is fructified by the surrounding world, by the masculine principle. The urban consciousness represented by Elsa is to be fructified by Lohengrin, by the Holy Grail. The connection between Lohengrin and Elsa von Brabant is the connection of material culture with [the spiritual task of] the fifth sub-race. The Swan is the initiate of the third grade who introduces the master from the Great Lodge. Human beings must allow the master to work on them without asking about his nature. Elsa von Brabant must regard what he gives her as being appropriate for her. The moment she starts asking about it out of curiosity, the initiate vanishes. This is all in the Lohengrin story.

The initiation wisdom of the Holy Grail had been brought over by the Knights Templar from the Orient to the Mountain of Salvation, *Mons salvationis*, Christendom's sacred site of initiation. An initiation ceremony pointed directly to the future of the whole human race. It was said that a time will come when Christianity will experience a new phase.

From time immemorial the onward course of human spiritual culture has been consciously determined by the progression of the sun. For around 2200 years before 800 BC the sun passed through the constellation of Taurus. During that period the divine was worshipped in Asia as the Bull. Even before that, for the same reason, Gemini was worshipped in Persia: good and evil—duality. Around 800 BC the sun entered the sign of Aries, or the Lamb. This is indicated by the legend of Jason and the Golden Fleece. Christ calls himself the Lamb of God because he appeared during this sign. [Today the sun is in the sign of Pisces.] The Templars pointed to the next constellation: the sun will then enter the constellation of Aquarius. Only then will Christianity really unfold, paganism will be connected with Christianity. This culture will awaken a new John. This moment will come when the sun is in the sign of Aquarius. John signifies Aquarius; he will be the proclaimer of a new age of Christianity. It is said that the Templar knights were referring to John the Baptist, not to Christ. But the John they are speaking about is the Water Carrier, Aquarius.

The last phase of Christianity that stems from the initiate Lohengrin, brought about the period of utilitarianism, which has now reached its zenith. The theosophical movement aspires to be the successor of such movements as the Parzival-movement and the one that spread out from the initiate Lohengrin. Even modern materialism has its origin in great initiates, but it must be superseded by a new phase, a new cycle. Theosophy aspires to bring this about. But it is always the initiates who are speaking when a new impulse is to be given to civilization.

Public Lecture

NUREMBERG, 2 DECEMBER 1907

Richard Wagner and his Relation to Mysticism

THEOSOPHY, or spiritual science, is not intended to be one-sided, satisfying only human inquisitiveness or a thirst for knowledge, but is meant to be a spiritual stream called upon to have a profound influence on everything we call the civilization of the present and the near future. We will get a feeling that theosophy might be capable of such a calling when we see how the impulses alive in it are, fundamentally speaking, to be found not only in this theosophy but are evident in our time as a more or less distinct presentiment in the most diverse fields.

Today we will look at how, in one of the greatest artists of modern times, there lived a similar element to that which we find in what we call theosophy, spiritual science. One should not think that everything I shall have to say about this significant artist of modern times, Richard Wagner, lived in him in his clear, rational consciousness. It would be an easy objection to say: 'You tell us all sorts of things pertaining to Richard Wagner, but we can prove that he never thought in these terms about himself.' This is an objection that anyone who considers Richard Wagner as we are doing today, can easily raise. It is not contended in any way that what will be said here lived in Wagner as distinct ideas. Whether one has the right to state such a thing is another question. It would take too much time to go in detail into how this right is derived. But a comparison, an image, can prove the justification for our considerations.

Does a botanist not think about plants? Does he not look for the laws by which they grow and live? Does he not understand thereby the nature of the plant, or seek to understand it? And since the plant does not itself have these laws in its consciousness, would someone be justified in denying the botanist the right to talk about the plant in this way? If we go more deeply into this image, we will see that what will be said today relates to the artist in the same way. It is not that we will simply repeat here the general notion that artists create unconsciously. But the laws by which, from a certain perspective of the world, we understand the artist, need no more be expressly defined by the consciousness of the artist than do the laws of growth by the plant. Let this be said right at the start to forestall the kind of objection just mentioned.

Another objection that can very easily arise at the present time is associated with the word *mysticism*. Recently in a small circle of people the word 'mysticism' was mentioned, and a somewhat erudite gentleman said that Goethe was actually also a mystic for he admitted that there is much in the world of human knowledge that remains dark and foggy. This showed that what the man understood by mysticism when practised by individuals, was all notions connected with what is foggy, unclear, dark. No genuine mystic ever understood mysticism to be something unclear, [something] we can only apprehend or have an inkling of in a general feeling way. Today we can hear it said in learned circles that what we know with clarity only reaches to a certain point; after that we begin to sink into the secrets of nature with general feelings, and that's where mysticism begins. On the contrary: what the genuine mystic sees in mysticism is that which is clearest of all, which can shine into the depths of existence with concepts bright as the sun. And when people talk about the darkness of mysticism, of all sorts of vague notions, this only means they have not made the effort to make clear for themselves what mysticism gives with clarity. In the first centuries of Christianity this was called *mathesis*, not because it was supposed to be mathematics, but because the ideas and thoughts formed by mysticism were supposed to be as clearly transparent as the concepts of mathematics. We just have to have patience to find our way into what true mysticism is. Let the word *mysticism* be associated with the name of Richard Wagner only in this sense.

Let us now characterize what the fundamental conviction is of every spiritual scientist: It is that behind our physical sense-perceptible world there is an invisible world, and that the human being is capable of penetrating into this invisible world. What this premise encompasses includes mysticism.

Did Wagner ever express such a conviction? Indeed, he did so clearly! And most importantly he expressed it from his perspective as a musician, indicating that for him music, art, was more than just an adjunct to existence, that for him it was the most important element of life. Where he talks of symphonic music he says wonderful words about art. He says that all symphonic music[86] appears as a revelation from another world, which elucidates for us the interconnections of existence in a completely different way from how logic is able to elucidate them, and that it is the most wonderful thing when we open ourselves to the convictions that throng to us in the elements of symphonic language; they then give us a certainty of feeling which the intellect's conclusions about the world cannot oppose.

We just need to realize that these are not words mentioned casually, but must be seen as an attempt to characterize something that comes from the most earnest depths of a great human understanding. Can we associate these words with the fundamental convictions of mysticism? Yes, indeed! If you research how mystics describe their process of coming to know something, you find for example the following statement, not in arbitrary terms but as something you can find as a sort of technical expression of mystics. Mystics say: In ordinary human cognition, man relies on his intellect to understand the laws of nature and of the spiritual world. But there is a higher form of knowing in which we do not link concept with concept in the manner of the intellect, but the ideas weave together like spiritual music—this is a different way of acquiring understanding. The true mystic knows the greater certainty of this method of knowing than is to be found in the judgements of the intellect in this area. And it is curious, but every individual who really knows, will describe this way of acquiring knowledge by using the image—it is more than an image!—of music. It is not just an image when in the ancient Pythagorean school they spoke of the music of the spheres.

Shallow academic philosophy regards the music of the spheres as an image, as a comparison with something. But one who knows what it is really about, also knows that the Pythagorean music of the spheres is a reality, and that there is a training of the mind and spirit whereby the sounds of this music can be heard.

It has often been said that we are surrounded by worlds of a spiritual kind that initially we cannot see, just as a blind person is surrounded by a world of colour which they don't see. When their eyes are operated on, brilliance and colour and light, which were previously not available, now open up to them. Such an opening of the spiritual capacity of sight also exists. It is just a matter of opening the higher senses, then the higher worlds appear out of the darkness. And we call the closest world that surrounds us the *light world* or *astral world*, and the next higher world is the actual spiritual world of the music of the spheres. This is a reality the human being can be born into through a kind of higher birth, just as the blind person can become sighted when operated on.

Those who are initiated speak undisguisedly of this world. We only have to think of Goethe's words. Certainly, many will regard what is about to be said as something fantastical; they will even regard it as unartistic to say such things because, with regard to an understanding of his work, they would rather leave the poet floating in vagueness. But a great poet like Goethe does not use empty phrases when he is trying to describe something specific, when he says, 'The sun sounds forth in ancient wise . . .' This is either pointing to something profound, or it is just a phrase, since the physical sun doesn't sound. And we should not assume an empty phrase of this nature in a poet like Goethe who worked from perception. As an initiate, Goethe knows that such a sounding world exists, a spiritually sounding world, and he holds to this image. And when in Part One he has Faust lifted up, after his aberrations, into the spiritual world, again we find:

> The new day is already born
> Sounding forth for spirit ears.

Goethe keeps fully to this image when he wants to describe the spiritual world.

For Richard Wagner, the sounds of external music were an expression, a revelation, of an inner music, of the world of spiritual sounding in the harmony pulsating through the world. He sensed this; he felt it. He said this himself more than once. Where he describes the individual instruments, he says:

> The primal organs of creation and of nature are represented in the instruments; what they express can never be clearly defined and fixed, for they reflect the primal feelings themselves as they emerged from the chaos of the first creation, when perhaps human beings did not even yet exist who could receive them into their heart.[87]

Our approach to these words should not be too intellectual; we must try to receive the full mood of them, then we feel how Richard Wagner's whole soul was immersed in what was called true genuine mysticism.

This is how Wagner saw his whole artistic mission. He is not an artist who merely wants to give expression to whatever happens to be living in his soul. He tries to sense what is required from the place where he finds himself in the course of evolution. He looks back into primal distances of humanity's past, into the human past when what we call art did not yet exist. Here we touch on a profound point which occupied Wagner continuously in his sense of mission, the same point that Nietzsche contemplated so deeply and tried to describe in his work *The Birth of Tragedy out of the Spirit of Music.*[88] We won't pursue what Nietzsche wrote, however, but will rather look to music, for it can tell us more than Nietzsche was able to bring to consciousness with regard to Richard Wagner. It takes us back to primal conditions of human development.

What were the mysteries? All the peoples of antiquity—the Egyptians, the Greeks and so on—had mystery centres which could equally be called temples as schools. Everywhere the *mysterium* contained the foundation of a later culture, and also, simultaneously, religion, science, and art. Let us try in rough outline to imagine ourselves in the nature of such a mysterium. What did someone experience there who, having passed certain tests, had been admitted to hear the mysteries? They experienced something which emerged later in the course of development in three separate branches—religion, art, and science—but which in the mysteries were [still] one in their [common] root. Imagine yourself as a beholder and listener in the mysterium! Let us take the case of how in the mysterium the riddle of the world was presented to the human individual. It was depicted how spiritual forces descended, how they live in the mineral, in the plant, how they become more perfect in the animal, and how they become self-conscious in man. The whole course of the cosmic spirit was depicted in such a way that eyes could see it all. And what eyes saw, ears heard, in colour, in light, in tone—this was wisdom, knowledge. These people, unlike today, did not take in by means of abstract ideas what is contained in cosmic laws. It was depicted: they saw it happen. The depiction was also beautiful at the same time. Thus art arose. Truth was given in the form of art. And they were absorbed in art in such a way that the human heart came into a religious mood and sank down in adoration.

This was present in the primal condition of every great culture. External history knows little about this and denies it. But no matter. In twenty years it will no longer deny such things. And just as these three were united in the original mysteries, so art, or the arts that later took separate paths, was a whole. Music and dramatic portrayal were united as one, and Wagner looked back to a primal time when the arts were united, presenting a totality. It was clear to him that because of the course human development had to take, the arts had had to go separate ways. But now in his time, so he believed, the epoch had come when a reuniting had to take place. He believed himself called upon, in the sphere of his abilities, to bring about a reunion of the separated streams, which he called a 'total work of art' (*Gesamtkunstwerk*). He felt that a true work of art should have the breath of a religious tinge in it. Thus for him a work of art was also religious service. We must think of all this in his feeling, and try to sense it ourselves. If we follow his thought in detail we will recognize it once more. Thus in his mind he saw a dramatic and musical work coming together out of these separate streams. He regarded Shakespeare and Beethoven as great artists. He saw in Shakespeare a dramatist who, with a wonderful inner coherence, brought human actions onto the stage in a way expressed in outer events. He saw in Beethoven an artist who was able to portray with the same wonderful inner coherence what took place internally in the breast, what did not pass over into external action, into gesture. And now he said to himself: This is something we can follow very precisely but which has to remain unspoken. For between one action and another there is something in the human breast that serves as a mediator, but which cannot [itself] change into the form of dramatic art. And when inner human feeling is expressed in a symphony, it has to remain held in itself, as it were, when the musician is required to remain in tone. We see in Beethoven's Symphony No. 9 how what is living inwardly in the soul finally finds its way out and becomes language [i.e. in the choral section of the last movement], wants to unite what is divided in art but, in human nature, belongs together as one whole.

This was Wagner's feeling about his mission. His idea of a 'total work of art' arose from it, which was to place the human being within art as a *whole* being. He should be within it experiencing his inner nature, and he should have the possibility of letting what lives so inwardly emerge outwardly as action. What cannot be expressed externally as drama can be supplied by music. What music cannot express emerges as external drama. Richard Wagner represents a synthesis of Shakespeare and Beethoven. This is Wagner's fundamental idea—a fundamental idea that is drawn deeply from the innermost nature of the human being. This is what he felt his mission to be. But now art had been shown a way into the innermost of human nature. Richard Wagner could not be an everyday dramatist. It had to be possible to portray the most profound things a human being can experience through the highest means of art—as once in the mysterium.

When we realize how, in symphonic music, Wagner sees the revelation of an unknown world, how he sees primal organs of creation in the various instruments, we soon begin to see how he feels it to be necessary to reveal more of the human being in his music dramas than we find here in the physical world. This [in the physical world] is only a part of human nature. Overarching this part is the higher man that lives in every person's inner being and which is far more than can be outwardly expressed. This higher man that surrounds the ordinary individual as though in encompassing glory, is more deeply connected with the wellsprings of life than can be clearly evident externally. But in wanting to make a connection with this higher human nature, Wagner cannot use ordinary everyday individuals: he must have recourse to those found in mythology. The figures in myth are depicted as growing beyond themselves; they are, and wish to be, far greater than a person of the physical plane could or would wish to be. Thus also connected with Wagner's mission is the fact that he goes beyond the everyday person and brings myth onto the stage. At the same time, using myth, Wagner must allow—albeit not in an intellectual way—the deeper world laws, the laws and beings of the unknown world, to be illuminated by the dramatic action, by the musical element. And this he does.

Naturally we cannot go into all the details; we can only take single examples. It will be evident everywhere how in his deepest being Wagner is connected with what spiritual science has to tell us about the world. For example, what does mysticism have to tell us about the social coexistence of human beings? For external observation people are juxtaposed; it sees individuals having effects on other individuals in the physical world when they talk to one another, becoming dependent on one another. But there are deeper connections in human nature. What lives as soul in one breast has a deep relationship with what lives as soul in another breast. And the laws that are evident on the surface are only the most insignificant ones. The deep network of laws that lies behind the soul goes from individual to individual. This is revealed by spiritual science. This is sensed by the artist. This is why he chooses subject matter by which he can show how there is a deeper law at work between person and person than can be seen by the external eye.

Straight away in one of his first works Richard Wagner shows us this urge to present mysterious connections. For do we not feel something of what moves invisibly between one person and another when the Dutchman appears with Senta? Are we not reminded of the wonderful connections in *Poor Henry*,[89] where the sacrifice of a pure maiden has a redemptive effect? We need to see such pictures as the expression of a deeper truth. This is something more true than the superficial truth of ordinary erudition. There is something real in the sacrifice a person makes for another. In this mystical bond, which is unintelligible to the superficial intellect, it comes to expression for example when we speak clearly of the 'All-soul'. This contains what comes to expression in an image of deepest truth, when one person does something for another.

I will now say something that spiritual science is able to demonstrate, so as to make this somewhat clearer for you. We know that the world evolves and that during the course of evolution some beings are always discarded. There is a law taught by spiritual science which says that every evolution to a higher level is connected with a decline to a lower level. Later, a balancing-out takes place. For every saint a sinner must arise. It requires a necessary equilibrium. It sounds very strange, but it is true. It is like when a fluid is mixed of two elements. If we want the one to be clearer, the other one has to become murkier. This is how it is with ascent. Every rise is connected with a fall. This necessitates that the being that has risen must use his power to redeem the other, the lower being. If there were not this interaction between beings there would be no development in the world. It brings evolution into flow. And when we see how one person sacrifices themself for another, we are reminded of just such a mysterious bond that arose because one being evolved higher and the other fell lower. Such a thing can only be tentatively hinted at. Thus Richard Wagner is already in the midst of the mysterious bond that goes from soul to soul.

When we look at his various works, we find that Wagner always drew his basic facts from mystical life. Let's look at his central work, his work on Siegfried, on the Nibelungs. In order to see how deeply they are drawn from world wisdom, we need to refer to something that theosophy makes fully clear, no matter how much it contradicts present-day science. Our far-distant ancestors inhabited a region of land to the west of Europe, between Africa and America. Even science is gradually realizing that there was land there once, the land we call Atlantis. Our very ancient ancestors lived there, albeit in very different form. As mentioned, science today is beginning to talk about this Ancient Atlantis. In the periodical *Kosmos*, published under the aegis of Haeckel, there was an article on this subject.[90] Certainly it only discusses what kind of animals and plants lived there. Of the fact that man also lived there, there is no mention as yet.

Things of which science now has an inkling are spoken about with clarity in spiritual science. There was a completely different atmosphere in Atlantis, completely different conditions. What we know today as the separation of sunshine and water in the air did not exist at that time. Over there, in the West, the air was permanently full of water vapour, of mist masses. The sun and moon could only be seen in a rainbow-like halo. The life of soul was also completely different. The way people lived was such that they had a far more inward connection with nature, with stone, plant, and animal. They were embedded in the masses of mist. True is the word: The Spirit of God moved upon the face of the waters. For what was preserved as an echo in the peoples descended from the Atlanteans, was all the more the case in the Atlanteans themselves—they understood everything around them. The trickling of a spring was not inarticulate, it was the expression of the wisdom of nature. People heard wisdom coming from all things in their surroundings, for these surroundings brought it about that these ancient ancestors were dimly clairvoyant. They did not perceive what was spread out in space but saw colour phenomena. They had clairvoyant forces. There was wisdom weaving in the mists and they perceived this wisdom with their dim forces. One can only give an indication of this. In the course of further development the mists precipitated as water and the air became clearer and clearer. Through this man evolved to this present state of consciousness. He became closed off from external nature, he became a being enclosed in himself. When man is still living in union with nature, wisdom is uniform, he lives in a sphere of wisdom; and this is the foundation of a certain brotherliness, for everyone perceives the same wisdom, everyone lives in the soul of the other. With the descent of the mist masses the human being entered into egotistical consciousness, into I-consciousness, where each person feels their own centre in themselves, where each person is confronted by the other and asserts their own domain. Brotherliness turns into the struggle for survival.

Myths and legends are not what academic analyses maintain them to be. What are legends and myths? They are the remnants of the ancient clairvoyant experiences of our ancestors. That is a fact. Assertions that myths signify a battle of one people against another, are nonsense. Academics talk about poetic folk-imagination. They just have to get to know a people and see whether they poetically change clouds into gods. They are just pulling the wool over people's eyes; it's fantasy, daydreaming. Even today you can still get a good idea of how legends arise. There are legends that are alive still today. For example, in various regions there is the legend of 'Lady Midday'. The legend tells that when field labourers stay in the fields at midday rather than having a break from field work and going home, Lady Midday will come to them and start posing questions. If they are unable to answer the questions by a certain time, she strangles them.[91] Who would not see a dream picture here of what happens to someone who lies out in the heat of the sun? Dreaming is the last remnant of the consciousness of that time. Here we see how even today a legend arises from a dream.

This is how all the Germanic myths and legends arose that have been preserved for us. These are primarily myths and legend that arose among the last stragglers from Atlantis. Thus the ancient Teutons remembered the time when their ancestors were over in the West—they did not come from the East—and how they migrated eastwards at the time when the mists of the Atlantean mistlands condensed and caused the floods known as the Flood [or Noah's Flood], how the air became clear, and the clear day-consciousness of the present emerged. The ancient Teuton looked back to the land of mists, to Nifelheim, and said: We have advanced from Nifelheim to the present world.

But there are certain spiritual beings who have remained behind at the spiritual stage that was right at that time. They are those which, with all their understanding, have preserved the character, the nature of Nifelheim, of the Nibelungs' home, and intrude into our time where they become 'spirits' because they no longer have a physical body. We have here a wonderful interweaving of strands. At no point should we approach this pedantically. We must take into account how imagination and clairvoyant ability—legend and fact—interweave.

We must not brush the dew from them, for they have to have it. People remembered how the mists precipitated, and then had the idea that when the mists sank, they formed the rivers of Northern and Central Europe. In the waters of the Rhine people saw something like a remnant of the mists of old Atlantis flowing along. And how did things progress? People had perceived wisdom in the trickling of springs. This was a wisdom they had in common, a shared element that excluded egoism. Now a very ancient symbol for wisdom is gold. So what became of this gold? It became a possession of the human I. What had previously been a shared wisdom whispered to people by Nature, now became a wisdom issuing from human discernment, from the I, [a wisdom] which the individual as an independent being came up against. Now the human being fashioned a 'ring' around himself. Through this ring the old brotherliness became embroiled in strife of people against each other. Wisdom as a shared element lived in the great legends of earlier times in the waters, and the last remnant, in the Rhine. That is where this wisdom had sunk.

But people have evolved to the point of egotistical consciousness. Even the Nibelungs had to develop ego-consciousness. They grabbed to themselves what had been shared, and made [from it] the ring that encompassed them as the ring of egoism. Here we see—expressed in somewhat sketchy terms—how true facts flow into the world of imagination, and how gold, the remnant of ancient wisdom that had reigned in the mists, how the wisdom-filled I fashions the ring about itself which gives rise to the struggle for survival. This is the deeper basis of the myth of the Nibelung horde.

This is something Wagner could give expression to in the great dramatic action and the tones of his music, which bring to expression an invisible world behind the visible. Thus he creatively transposed the Nibelung legend into a modern form, and gave us this whole developmental process in his Nibelung work. We feel how the new gods who reign over humankind have found their transition from the old gods.

Let us think ourselves back to Ancient Atlantis—clouds of mist where wisdom spoke everywhere out of all things. Now powers had to arbitrate between people, no longer leading by means of common wisdom but through covenants and commandments, and had even fixed the gods in covenants. This had its origin in a primordial, wisdom-filled consciousness. When the new god Wotan is at a crucial point, when Fafner is supposed to give back Freya, where Wotan himself is restricted by ego-wisdom, by the ring, the ancient sacred consciousness of humanity comes once more before him, the consciousness of the earth that enfolded humanity when it still lived on Atlantis. The consciousness of that time, in which everything was embedded, is portrayed in Erda: her sleep is dreaming, her dreaming is contemplation, her contemplation is the sway of knowledge.[92] This contains a cosmological truth. This truth is in everything, has created everything. It is alive in springs, rustles in leaves, wafts in the wind. There it finds the human I. There it was an all-encompassing consciousness from which all individual consciousness has arisen: the sway of knowledge. Old clairvoyance was a reflection of this reigning knowledge. Then the human being was not enclosed in his skin. Consciousness pervaded everything. One couldn't say then that ego-consciousness was here or there—it was embedded in everything. Wagner's intuition shows this wonderfully:

> You know
> What the deeps hide,
> What pervades hill and dale,
> Air and water;
> Where beings are
> There wafts your breath;
> Where brains brood,
> There your mind is:
> All things, men say,
> Are known to you.[93]

Everything is known to Erda through this consciousness. And so, step by step, we are able to see everywhere how what Wagner put intuitively into the Nibelung myth, appears for us like an imprint of primordial world wisdom.

Let us imagine ourselves—and it needs to be repeated that Wagner himself did not do this with conscious intellect—at the time of the transition from the old stage of development to the new.

Over in Atlantis there was a brotherhood-consciousness. Then came the transition to ego-consciousness, the quality of independence in human nature. And let's imagine ourselves at the beginning of *Rheingold*. Do we not hear the element of ego-consciousness in the first notes, in the long chord in E-flat major? And do we not sense how this separate consciousness rises up out of a more general consciousness? Thus through Wagner's own knowledge, and motif by motif, we could find that a world hidden behind the world's phenomena reveals itself in the musical sound, and that in practice he uses the instruments as archetypal organs of nature. I would not wish to present Wagner to you as someone embodying a vague mysticism. His artistic creativity is immersed in the essence of a mystical clarity.

And when we pass from this to another work, to *Lohengrin*, how does what mysticism has to give play into the picture here? Lohengrin is the messenger of the Holy Grail, who comes from the place of initiates where high wisdom reigns. The Lohengrin legend has a connection with the legends we find everywhere that show us how initiates intervene in ordinary human nature. Everywhere, at important moments in development, we are made aware of legend, which is deeper than history. Our attention is directed to how such initiate forces intervene in the course of history. Legend does not give us an external succession of events.

The transition from general consciousness to individual consciousness was a significant time. The Lohengrin myth tries to describe this change. We see it is a time when a new spirit struggles free from the old. Two spirits of the time face one another. This is depicted in the conflict between the two women. Elsa, the feminine element, always represents the soul struggling towards what is highest. Banal interpretations cannot be applied to what Goethe wrote in his 'Chorus mysticus': 'The Eternal-Feminine draws us on'. This was written out of the most profound mysticism. The soul must be fructified by the great events through which new principles enter into development. What enters is portrayed in the initiates who come from places of significance. Here spiritual science speaks about advanced individuals. One is always asked: Why don't they show themselves? If they revealed themselves, they would not be acknowledged. People would ask them about their ordinary bourgeois name and class. But for someone working out of the spiritual world this is the most insignificant thing. An initiate whose task it is to make known the great mysteries is so high beyond things like birth, name, class, profession, that it makes no sense to ask him about them. Where questions like this are posed, the understanding for his profound mission is so remote that a separation has to take place.

> You should never ask me
> Nor worry about knowing
> Whence my journey brought me.
> Nor what my name is or my standing.[94]

If asked about their name and background, any of those who do not live in just the ordinary world could reply with Lohengrin's words. This is one of the notes that is sounded in *Lohengrin*, where genuine clear mysticism shines a light into the life of music and drama.

There is in the world a profound secret, a mystery, possessed by humanity. It is depicted symbolically in a legend that has to be deeply understood: When the spirit who, at the beginning of our evolution, fell from the spirits guiding humanity, when Lucifer fell, a stone fell from his crown, and from this stone was fashioned a chalice—the chalice used by Christ Jesus and his disciples at the Last Supper, the chalice with which Joseph of Arimathea collected the blood at Golgotha and brought it to the West. After many journeyings, the chalice came into the hands of Titurel, who founded the Grail Castle. Titurel preserved it along with the sacred Lance of Love. The legend tells us that all who look into the chalice receive into themselves something of an eternal element.

Let's understand the whole mystery of this legend: a harmony with the progress of human development as seen by those who know of the mystery of the Grail. They said: When human development began on earth, all love was connected with the blood. It was blood relationships that tied people together. We find small tribes in which marriage to close relatives was predominant. Only later did marriage to non-relatives emerge. The moment when marriage outside the tribe is permitted marks a significant transition in the life of every tribe.

An awareness of this is preserved in myths and legends. So initially love was tied to blood relationships; then the circles in which one could marry grew wider and wider. This is the one stream in development: love that is bound up with equality and community of flesh and blood. Then another principle became decisive, which implanted independence. In those ancient times preceding Christianity—so said the Grail knights—there were these two streams: love tied to blood-brotherhood, and the freedom principle, that which prevails in the human being as an independent element, as a luciferic element, the power of Yahveh whose name means 'I am that I am'. In Christianity a love was to be brought into the world that was independent of blood-brotherhood. This is how the words of Christ are to be interpreted: Whoever does not leave father and mother cannot be my disciple. This means: Whoever is not able to replace love tied to flesh and blood with a general love of humanity, which moves from soul to soul, from individual to individual in general, and which must gradually develop, cannot be my disciple.

Thus we see that the chalice falls from Lucifer's crown. It unites the Lucifer-principle with the Christ-principle. This knowledge brought to the Grail knights the great energy that permeated them with ego-life. We find this meaning in the legend of the Holy Grail. And the following was explained to the pupils of the Holy Grail. I will present in the form of simple dialogue what gradually became clear to the Grail pupils over long periods of practice. Many will say it is unbelievable. But it is the same with truth as with ambassadors of civilized nations to the courts of barbarians—as Voltaire said: They have to suffer unworthy treatment before they are accepted.

So the Grail pupil was told the following: Look at the plant. Its flower cannot be compared with the human head; with its male and female organs of reproduction the flower corresponds with the sexual aspect of the human being. The root corresponds to the human head. Darwin has already correctly indicated in a comparison, that the root corresponds to the head in human beings.[95] The human being is a reversed plant; he has made a complete turn. The plant stretches its calyx chastely towards the light, absorbing its rays, the holy Lance of Love, receiving its pure kiss, under which the fruit forms. The turn is half accomplished in the animal. The plant that penetrates with its head into the soil, the animal with its horizontal spine, and the human being with his upright gait, his gaze directed upwards (Steiner draws on the board)—these three together make a cross. Just see—the pupil was told—how Plato was making known the truth when he said that the world-soul is spread out, is crucified on the body of the world.[96] The world-soul, the soul that moves through plant, animal, and man, is found in the bodies that depict a cross. This is the original meaning of the cross. Everything else is just talk.

What is the result of this reversal in the human being? When we consider the plant we see that, for the genuine mystic, the plant has the state of consciousness of a sleeping person. When he sleeps, a person is the same worth as a plant. The human being has gained his present-day consciousness by pervading his pure, chaste plant-body with desire, with the body of passions. Through this he has, in a certain sense, advanced to self-awareness, but he has bought this at the price of permeating his pure plant-substance with desires and urges. And now a future condition of the human being was painted for the pupil, a condition where the human being will have retained his bright consciousness but, purified and cleansed, will have reverted once more to pure substance like a plant. He will then have won back a pure chaste nature. The organ of reproduction will be transformed. One pictured, from the viewpoint of the Grail knights, that the human being of the future will have organs that serve reproduction in such a way that they will not be permeated by desire, but will be pure and chaste like a flower calyx turning to the Lance of Love, to the sun's ray. Thus the ideal of the Grail will be realized—when man brings forth his own kind in chaste purity like the plants, when he generates his own likeness in the pure higher calyx, when the human being becomes a creator in spirit. This real ideal was called the Grail, the transformed human reproductive organs that bring forth a human being as purely and chastely as the larynx today brings forth the word by activating vibrations in the air.

We will now try to show how this great ideal was living in Wagner's mind. On Good Friday in 1857 he was standing on the balcony of

Frau Wesendonck's garden house, looking at the shoots of the first plants. He made a note of this memorable moment. In the sprouting forth of the young plants he felt the whole mystery of the Holy Grail, the coming-to-birth of everything connected with the idea of the Holy Grail. He felt this in connection with Good Friday. A wonderful feeling came over him. And the first thought of his *Parsifal* shot into his mind. A great deal more came to him in the time that followed; but the feeling remained. He developed his figure of Parsifal from it, the figure in whom feeling is raised to knowledge, where one becomes 'knowing through compassion'. And we see in the Amfortas mystery the whole phase in which human nature becomes wounded by the impure lance. We see how the mystical mystery of the Holy Grail is illumined here.

This is not something that may be touched on with rough hands. One has to follow the whole feeling, and hold in mind the ideas in their totality. Everywhere we look we see how, although Wagner did perhaps not think mystically, as an artist and human being he presented everything he did in a mystical light. That is the crux of the matter.

Spiritual science is not supposed to give us theory but something that becomes immediate life. This too is how Wagner clearly felt his mission, so clearly, so mystically, that he could say: The kind of art that lives as an ideal in me must once again become divine service. He had sensed the flowing-together once more of the three streams, and wanted to be an emissary of their joint activity himself. From his mystical knowledge there follows what has lived as a mystical and clear feeling in all the great masters, and what we feel when we make a connection between the great masters and mysticism. Goethe sensed it. The human being then becomes healthy again, feels something of that by which he overcomes himself when he experiences what is in 'Die Geheimnisse':

> The human being who overcomes himself
> Frees himself from the power that binds all beings.[97]

When this mood of becoming free of the I, of living into the mysteries of the cosmos, pulsates through all our energies, then is the human being a mystic in all areas. Whether externally in religion or science or art—he wrestles to bring himself into a unity in the sense of a unified human nature. This is what Goethe wanted to articulate as the secret of every whole human being, when he summarized the secret of his own soul in the words:

> One who has science and art also has religion.
> If he has neither of these, let him have religion.[98]

Notes

Textual sources:

24 June, 1, 8, 15, and 22 July 1904: notes taken by Marie Steiner-von Sivers and Franz Seiler.

30 September 1904: notes taken by Marie Steiner-von Sivers.

14 October 1904: notes taken by Marie Steiner-von Sivers and Franz Seiler.

21 and 28 October 1904: notes taken by Marie Steiner-von Sivers, Mathilde Scholl and Franz Seiler.

28 March and 5 May 1905: notes taken by Marie Steiner-von Sivers and Walter Vegelahn.

12 May 1905: notes taken by Walter Vegelahn and Eugenie von Bredow.

3 December 1905: notes taken by Mathilde Scholl.

2 December 1907: transcript by Georg Klenk.

Titles of the individual lectures are those given by the stenographers to their transcripts.

1 This is a reference to the lecture on 10 June 1904 'Der Gegensatz von Kain und Abel' (The polarity of Cain and Abel), in *The Temple Legend*, GA 93.

2 A theosophical conference took place in Amsterdam from 19 to 21 July 1904. Rudolf Steiner wrote a detailed account of this in the magazine 'Lucifer-Gnosis', printed in *Lucifer-Gnosis*, GA 13.

3 The period of Old Moon which preceded our Earth evolution, as described in the chapter on 'World Evolution and the Human Being' in Rudolf Steiner's *Occult Science*, GA 13.

4 Steiner speaks in detail about the pitris (the name means *fathers*) in the Berlin lecture of 1 October 1905, in GA 93a (*Foundations of Esotericism*).

5 King of the Huns whose empire stretched at one time from the Black Sea to the Rhine. He was called a cruel ruler and 'the Scourge of God' by the later, Christianized Germanic people.

6 Veleda was a Germanic priestess and prophetess. The Roman writer

Tacitus records that in the first century of the Christian era she led the Bructeri tribe. She was captured by the Romans and taken to Rome. There she continued to prophesy, and was frequently revered as a goddess.

7 Wolfram von Eschenbach was an important German writer of the Middle Ages. His exact dates are not known (between 1170 and 1220). His greatest work is the epic *Parzival.*

8 'Hamsa' is an occult term for initiate. The word means 'swan'.

9 *Heinrich (Henry) I*, 876-936, was the first German king of the Saxony dynasty, which superseded the Carolingian line.

10 Gospel of John, 1:14.

11 Gospel of John, 14:6.

12 Lycurgus lived in the second half of the ninth century BCE. Plutarch (46-125 CE) describes his life in some detail in his parallel biographies where he contrasts a Greek statesman with a Roman one. Among other places, Lycurgus travelled to Crete to study the Cretan laws. He introduced many of these to Sparta. He then went to Delphi after getting the Spartans to swear not to change any of the laws he had given them until his return. However, he died before returning so the Spartans were bound by oath to keep his laws [unchanged]. See also Friedrich von Schiller's treatise *Die Gesetzgebung des Lykurgus und Solon* (The law-giving of Lycurgus and Solon).

13 In his later work, *The Laws (nomoi)*, there is a conversation between an Athenian, a Lacedaemonian, and a Cretan. Right in the first chapter the Athenian talks about the laws of Crete which are known throughout Greece and admired for their exemplary nature. Later on the wise law-giving of the mythical Cretan King Minos is often mentioned.

14 In Lecture 5 of the cycle *St John's Gospel*, GA 103, Steiner describes the seven grades of a certain form of occidental initiation. The sixth of these grades is called the 'Sun-runner' (*Sonnenläufer*).

15 *Archon*: translated as ruler, captain, chief, king. There were nine archons in Athens, newly elected each year. The first was the highest judge and was called *archon eponymos*, which means 'the name-giver', because the year was named after him. The second was in charge of religious services and festivals; he was called *archon basileus*, which means 'the king-ruler'.

16 *Herodotus*, around 485-425 BCE, Greek historian.

17 In order better to understand the following sentences, here are the main events associated with them (from Schlosser's *Weltgeschichte* ((World History)), Volume II): Alba Longa was founded by Ascanius, a descendant of Aeneas. His descendants ruled over the city for 14 generations, the last of which being Numitor who was expelled by his brother Amulius. Although Amulius let Numitor live, he exiled him from the city, killed his son, and forced his daughter Rhea Silvia to become a priestess of Vesta, who thus had to remain unmarried. But the god of war, Mars, secretly lay with her and she bore the twins Romulus and Remus. Amulius had the twins put into a basket and thrown into the River Tiber. A she-wolf found and suckled them. As an adult, Romulus built the city of Rome and became the progenitor of the seven kings of Rome. He slew his brother Remus for mocking the city while it was being built.

18 The sibyls were prophetesses in antiquity. One of these, the Cumaean sibyl, is the source of the Sibylline Books which were kept in the temple of Jupiter in Rome, and consulted at moments of crisis.

19 Tages, according to Roman mythology, was found by a farmer in a ploughed furrow, was as small as a boy but as wise as a sage. He taught the people divination by reading the entrails of sacrificed animals. This skill was called *haruspicy*.

20 *S*ee note 4.

21 *The Secret Doctrine*: see note 34.

22 Ceridwen: a nature goddess of the Druids. The cauldron of Ceridwen was the symbol of a particular order of bards in ancient Britain, the Order of the Cauldron, which had its own secrets and sang special songs at festivals. Steiner talks of Ceridwen in more detail in a public lecture in Berlin on 6 May 1909 'Die europäischen Mysterien und ihre Eingeweihten' (European mysteries and their initiates) (in GA 57), and also in Landin on 29 July 1906 in the lecture titled 'Das Gralsgeheimnis im Werk Richard Wagners' (The mystery of the Grail in the work of Richard Wagner) (in GA 97, *The Christian Mystery*).

23 Merlin is a mysterious figure of ancient British saga cycles (he was said to be the son of the devil and a nun). Merlin was connected with the Round Table of King Arthur.

24 Boniface (Winfrid) came from England but worked predominantly in

Germany to spread Roman Catholic Christianity. Born around 680, he was killed by Frisian pagans in 755 during a missionary journey to Frisia.

25 See note 7.

26 Helena Petrovna Blavatsky (1831-1891) and Colonel Henry Steel Olcott founded the Theosophical Society on 17 November 1875 in New York, but later moved its centre to Adyar in India.

27 John of Damascus (around 675-749) is regarded as a saint in both the Catholic and Greek Orthodox Churches. He wrote a systematic summary of Orthodox faith, also a work in defence of religious icons, and wrote many hymns. See also 'The Legend of Barlaam and Josaphat, attributed to Saint John of Damascus', translated [into German] from the Greek by Ludwig Burchard, Munich.

28 The Jataka collection is a book of tales about Buddha's previous existences. From Pali, an Indian idiom in which ancient religious writings are set down. Today it is only spoken by monks in Ceylon, Burma, and Thailand.

29 Steiner uses the term 'round' for the separate embodiments of the Earth, which are described in *Occult Science* as 'Old Saturn,' 'Old Sun,' 'Old Moon,' and 'Earth' (GA 13, chapter on 'The Evolution of the World and of Man').

30 Because of its content, this lecture is also printed in *The Temple Legend* (GA 93) and expanded there by an extract about the Druids and Scandinavian mysteries from the book *The Secret Societies of All Ages and Countries* by Charles William Heckethorn, which Rudolf Steiner had in his library.

31 In 61CE, the Romans, under the command of Suetonius Paulinus, conquered and destroyed the Druid religious centre on the island of Mona (the former name of the island of Anglesey in north-western Wales). The Roman writer Tacitus writes about it in the 14th book of his *Annals* (§ 29 and 30).

32 Steiner also spoke later about the Prometheus legend, for example in Lecture 10 in *Ägyptische Mythen und Mysterien* (*Egyptian Myths and Mysteries*), GA 106.

33 Steiner is referring to the preceding lectures. In addition to the ongoing branch meetings on Mondays, Steiner also spoke in June/July 1904 to a smaller group of people who met in the flat of Klara Motzkus in Char-

lottenburg. After a summer break in August, these meetings resumed in September/October.

34 Helena Petrovna Blavatsky (1831-1891) was co-founder, with Henry Steel Olcott, of the Theosophical Society in 1875. Her book *The Secret Doctrine* was published in 1888. A chapter of this book (in Volume II, 'Anthropogenesis', part one, stanza XII) is dedicated to Prometheus. Blavatsky writes about the meaning of the Prometheus legend as follows: 'The Titan is more than a thief of the celestial fire. He is the representation of humanity—active, industrious, intelligent, but at the same time ambitious, which aims at equalling divine powers. Therefore it is humanity punished in the person of Prometheus, but it is only so with the Greeks. With the latter, Prometheus is not a criminal, save in the eyes of the gods. In his relation with the Earth, he is, on the contrary, a god himself, a friend of mankind, which he has raised to civilization and initiated into the knowledge of all the arts; a conception which found its most poetical expounder in Aeschylus.'

35 Prometheus knows a prophesy that destruction and ruin lay ahead for Zeus, the father of the gods, through a new covenant of marriage.

36 The name derives from the Sanskrit root *man* = to think. In Indian and theosophical terminology it signifies high spiritual beings who have the task of developing new races. Concerning the manu of the fifth root-race, i.e. of the post-Atlantean era, see Steiner's *Aus der Akasha-Chronik* (From the akashic chronicle), GA 11, *Cosmic Memory*; and *Occult Science*, GA 13.

37 *The Story of Atlantis* by William Scott Elliot. See also chapter on 'Unsere atlantischen Vorfahren' (our Atlantean ancestors) in Steiner's *Aus der Akasha-Chronik* (From the Akashic Chronicle), GA 11, *Cosmic Memory*.

38 *Adam Kadmon*: See also Steiner's lecture in Oxford, 22 August 1922, in GA 214, *The Mystery of the Trinity*.

39 In the notes taken by Franz Seiler, we find the following unclear sentences: 'Every myth changes. They originate from most ancient primordial times and change at a particular point. This happens in every myth, also those that are to be taken literally.'

40 *Lucifer-Gnosis* was a periodical that had been published by Steiner in collaboration with Marie von Sivers since 1903. Initially it came out monthly, then increasingly more seldom. Due to the huge amount of unforeseen work Steiner had to deal with, the publication had to be discontinued in

1908. The articles, covering the evolution of the cosmos, the Earth, and humanity, were then compiled and published as a book with the title *The Akashic Chronicle*, GA 11(*Cosmic Memory*). The lectures mentioned here are discussed in the chapters on 'Our Atlantean Forebears' and 'The Fourth and Fifth Root-races'.

41 Thales of Miletus, 624-546 BCE; Anaximenes was active between 585 and 525 BCE; Socrates, around 470 to 399 BCE. Steiner discusses these and other philosophers of Greek antiquity in his book *The Riddles of Philosophy*, GA 18, in the chapter on 'The Worldview of the Greek Thinker'.

42 GA 8, *Christianity as Mystical Fact*. The interpretation of the legend of Odysseus is in the chapter on 'Mystery Wisdom and Myth'.

43 The inclination of this people to black magic and lower forms of sorcery is discussed in the first two lectures of the lecture cycle *The Gospel of St Matthew,* GA 123, particularly on pages 21-26 and 50-53.

44 'Gobi' is the Mongolian name, and 'Shamo' the Chinese name, for the great desert between East Turkestan, Dzungaria and Manchuria. Today it is politically divided between China, Xinjiang and Mongolia.

45 Steiner speaks on various occasions about the working of the Master Jesus in humanity's development, but particularly in the lecture cycle *The Gospel of St Luke*, GA 114.

46 'The Song of the Nibelungs' is an epic poem written in middle-high German around 1200 by an unknown author. The first part deals with Siegfried's life, his marriage to Kriemhild the queen of the Nibelungs, also called the 'Burgundian', and his murder by Hagen. The second part relates Kriemhild's marriage to Attila, the king of the Huns, and how with his help she gets her revenge by inviting all the kings of the Nibelungs to her court, where she kills them and all their retinue of heroes in a bloody battle.

47 First Letter of St John, 5:7.

48 In Nordic mythology, 'Gudrun' means the wife of Siegfried and the sister of the Burgundian king. In the middle-high German epic poem 'Die Nibelungen,' her name is then Kriemhild. The so-called *Gudrunlied* (song of Gudrun) or *Kudrunlied*, is part of a different saga cycle.

49 The opening line of the Song of the Nibelungs.

50 In Germanic antiquity studies the two terms, *Woden* and *Odin,* are considered to be names for one and the same god.

51 *Póntos Pyletós*: literally = narrow-strait sea.

52 *Selene* in ancient Greek means 'moon'.

53 This contest between the most significant minstrels of that time (Walther von der Vogelweide, Wolfram von Eschenbach, Heinrich von Ofterdingen and a few others) is reputed to have taken place at the castle, called the Wartburg, of the Count of Thuringia at the beginning of the thirteenth century. Richard Wagner used this event as the theme of his opera *Tannhäuser*.

54 Steiner speaks about Jakob Böhme (1575-1624) in detail in his book *Die Mystik im Aufgange des neuzeitlichen Geisteslebens* (*Mysticism at the Dawn of the Modern Age*), GA 7.

55 Friedrich Hölderlin, 1770-1843, in his novel *Hyperion oder der Eremit in Griechenland* (Hyperion or the hermit of Greece). The novel is about a Greek of the present who would like to renew the old way of life, close to the gods, of the past. He sees that the Greeks of his present are unable to do this, and looks for a way to realize his ideas in Germany. He has the experience there which is expressed in the quoted words.

56 *The Wibelungs*: Wagner worked intensively on this legend cycle and also on the legends about Frederick Barbarossa in the summer of 1848. He writes about it in an article, 'Die Wibelungen, Weltgeschichte aus der Sage' (The Wibelungs, world history in legends). This work later led to his four-part dramatic opera *The Ring of the Nibelungs*.

57 Took place in the year 800.

58 Frederick I, called Barbarossa ('Redbeard'), 1122-1190, ruled from 1152 to 1190. He took part in the second and third Crusade, and died during the latter.

59 A legend about Barbarossa said that he was not dead but was waiting in Kyffhäuser-Berg for the hour when he would rise again and rescue Germany.

60 Steiner discusses this process in more detail in his book *Aus der Akasha-Chronik* (The Akashic Chronicle) GA 11(*Cosmic Memory*), in the final chapter on 'Our Atlantean Ancestors'.

61 *Attila*: see note 5.

62 Leo I—pope from 440 to 461.

63 This refers to a place in *Siegfried* where Wotan/Odin tries to block the hero's way to Brunhild with his spear, but Siegfried uses his own sword, which he forged himself, to cut Wotan's spear in two (Act III: Scene 2).

64 Winfrid Boniface (Saint Boniface) c. 675-754 was an Anglo-Saxon Christian missionary to Germanic parts of the Frankish empire. He is said to have cut down the Donar Oak (Oak of Thor), a sacred tree of the Germanic pagans.

65 In the fourth and final scene of *Rheingold*, 'An open space on a mountain height'.

66 Scene I of *Götterdämmerung*, final song of the three Norns.

67 This is the final verse of the third and final Act of *Tristan and Isolde,* sung by Isolde before she dies.

68 Fourth sentence of the Catholic Creed.

69 *Parsifal*: In Wolfram von Eschenbach's epic, the name is spelt with z and v, i.e. Parzival. Wagner adopted the spelling 'Parsifal' from the scholar and writer Johannes Joseph von Görres. Görres maintains the origin of the name to be Persian, meaning 'the pure fool'. Wagner puts this meaning into the mouth of Kundry when she addresses Parsifal in Klingsor's enchanted garden with the words: 'I called you foolish pure one *(Fal parsi)*, you, pure fool Parsifal.' (Towards the end of Act 2.)

70 In his autobiographical work *A Communication to My Friends*, Wagner details the circumstances and thoughts that led him to consider such a plan, to write an outline of the drama, but then not to carry it out.

71 Hartmann von Aue's dates and origin are uncertain. He was probably born around 1165 and certainly died after 1210. Apart from 'Poor Henry' he also wrote many epics in verse form as well as minnelieds and Crusade songs.

72 The idea of Jerusalem as the centre of the world is referred to in the first verses of the second canto in 'Purgatory'. More details can be found in the notes by Ida and Walther von Warburg in the Manesse-Verlag's edition of the *Divine Comedy* (page 439).

73 This is probably referring to the following sentence: 'In this respect we have to regard it as a sublime attribute of the Christian religion that the profoundest truth was to be expressly open to the "poor in spirit", for their comfort and salvation; whereas, by contrast, the doctrine of the Brahmins was exclusively for "those who know", for which reason the "rich in spirit" looked on the nature-ridden multitude as excluded from the possibility of knowledge. . .'

74 In his prose work *Religion and Art*, Wagner connects 'the degeneration

of the human race' with the departure from the 'Brahminic doctrine on the sinfulness of killing living things'. He also refers to the newly arisen movements for vegetarianism, the societies for the protection of animals, and the temperance societies, but which, he said, 'in their fragmented state are completely ineffective'.

75 Steiner discusses this novel in the March 1905 edition of the periodical *Lucifer-Gnosis*, under the title of 'Flita: the true story of a female black magician.' The article is reprinted in GA 34, page 512.

76 Arthur Schopenhauer, 1788-1860.

77 Friedrich Nietzsche (1844-1900) was a personal friend of Wagner's for many years and to begin with had a positive attitude towards his artistic work. This is evident in his booklet *Richard Wagner in Bayreuth*. Then, in the years 1878-1880, he distanced himself entirely from the master of Bayreuth. His rejection is expressed in two works: *Wagner's Fall* and *Nietzsche contra Wagner*.

78 The Dionysia was a festival celebrated in the spring and autumn of each year in Greece in honour of the god Dionysus. The Great Dionysia, in March, was particularly important in Athens, during which tragedies and satyr plays were performed.
Aeschylus, 525-456 BCE.
Sophocles, 496-406 BCE.

79 Marie von Sivers, later Frau Marie Steiner, got to know both Édouard Schuré (1841-1929) and his plays at the end of the nineteenth century. It was through him that she became aware of the Theosophical Society and Rudolf Steiner. She translated some of Schuré's books into German. Steiner speaks in detail on the original drama at Eleusis in his article 'Aristoteles über das Mysteriendrama' (Aristotle on mystery drama), published in *Lucifer-Gnosis, gesammelte Aufsätze 1903-1908*, GA 34. Important discussion is also to be found in the volume *Marie Steiner-von-Sivers—Ein Leben für die Anthroposophie* (Marie Steiner-von-Sivers—a life for anthroposophy), page 69. The 'Drama of Eleusis' is in Schuré's book *Sanctuaires d'Orient*.

80 See note 64. By felling the oak sacred to the Germanic god Donar, Boniface was showing the victory of Christianity over pagan religon.

81 From the time of the Hohenstaufen kaisers (1138-1254), this is what the followers of the German kaiser were called, in contrast to the Guelphs,

who followed the Pope. Historians are uncertain as to the origin of the name, and opinions differ.

82 In Norse mythology, Vili and Ve were the brothers of Odin (Wotan).

83 The reference is to the Transfiguration recounted in the three Synoptic Gospels: Matthew 17:1-13; Mark 9:2-13; Luke 9:28-36.

84 From Goethe's *Faust*, Part One, verses 243-246. These words are spoken by Archangel Raphael at the beginning of the 'Prologue in Heaven'.

Die Sonne tönt nach alter Weise
In Brudersphären Wettgesang,
Und ihre vorgeschriebne Reise
Vollendet sie mit Donnergang.

85 From Goethe's *Faust*, Part Two, verses 4667-4674. Spoken by the air spirit Ariel.

Tönend wird für Geistesohren
Schon der neue Tag geboren.
Felsentore knarren rasselnd,
Phöbus Räder rollen prasselnd,
Welch Getöse bringt das Licht!
Es trommetet, es posaunet,
Auge blinzt und Ohr erstaunet,
Unerhörtes hört sich nicht.

86 See note 87.

87 The quote comes from the novella *Eine Pilgerfahrt zu Beethoven* (Pilgrimage to Beethoven). Between 1840 and 1841 Wagner was residing in Paris. At that time he published a work with the title *Ein deutscher Musiker in Paris. Novellen und Aufsätze* (A German Musician in Paris. Short Stories and Essays). It begins with the above-mentioned novella. It relates in poetic form how a young man travels on foot to Vienna so as to be able to talk to Beethoven. The story is very humorous, but also evinces a great reverence for the master. The quote is preceded by a comparison of orchestral music with a music produced by 'a more beautiful and noble organ of sound', 'the human voice.'

88 *Die Geburt der Tragödie aus dem Geiste der Musik. Oder Griechentum und Pessimismus* (The Birth of Tragedy out of the Spirit of Music. Or Hellenism

and Pessimism) by Friedrich Nietzsche, published in 1872, a new edition with the previously published *Versuch einer Selbstkritik* (An Attempt at Self-Criticism) 1886.

89 See note 71.

90 An article was published in 1905 in the periodical *Kosmos, Handweiser für Naturfreunde,* Volume 5, with the title 'Paläontologische Umschau' (Palaeontological Survey), describing the flora, fauna and principally the saurians of 'prehistory'.

91 Poludnitsa (Lady Midday or the Noon Witch) is a mythical character common to the various Slavic countries of Eastern Europe. She is only seen on the hottest part of the day and is a personification of a sunstroke.

92 Slightly adapted lines from Wagner's *Siegfried*, Act 3: Scene 1.
Erda:

My sleep is dreaming,
My dreaming is contemplation,
My contemplation is the sway of knowledge.

93 *Siegfried*, Act 3: Scene 1.
Wanderer (addressing Erda):

Bekannt ist dir was die Tiefe birgt,
was Berg und Thal, Luft und Wasser durchwebt:
wo Wesen sind, wehet dein Athem;
wo Hirne sinnen, haftet dein Sinn:
Alles sagt man, sei dir bekannt.

94 From *Lohengrin*, Act1:Scene 3.
Lohengrin:

Nie sollst du mich befragen,
Noch Wissens Sorge tragen,
Woher ich kam der Fahrt.
Noch wie mein Nam' und Art.

95 In *The Power of Movement in Plants,* at the end of the final chapter (Chapter 12), Darwin (1809-1882) writes:
'It is hardly an exaggeration to say that the tip of the radicle thus

endowed, and having the power of directing the movements of the adjoining parts, acts like the brain of one of the lower animals; the brain being seated within the anterior end of the body, receiving impressions from the sense-organs, and directing the several movements.'

96 Mentioned in Plato's *Timaeus,* Chapter 8. Steiner uses a formulation here of the Viennese philosopher, Vinzenz Knauer, whom Steiner knew personally, from his work *Die Hauptprobleme der Philosophie in ihrer Entwickelung und teilweisen Lösung von Thales bis Robert Hamerling* (The chief problem and partial solution of philosophy in its development from Thales to Robert Hamerling), Vienna and Leipzig 1892, page 96. This was in Steiner's library and underlined: 'In myth, according to the *Timaeus*, God had laid out this world-soul in the form of a cross throughout the universe, and stretched the world-body over it.'

97 The closing lines of Goethe's poem 'Die Geheimnisse' (The Mysteries):

Von der Gewalt, die alle Wesen bindet,
befreit der Mensch sich, der sich überwindet.

Steiner gave a whole lecture on this poem on 25 December 1907, in GA 98.

98 From *Zahme Xenien* by Goethe:

Wer Wissenschaft und Kunst besitzt, hat auch Religion.
Wer jene beiden nicht besitzt, der habe Religion.

RUDOLF STEINER'S COLLECTED WORKS

THE German Edition of Rudolf Steiner's Collected Works (the *Gesamtausgabe* [GA] published by Rudolf Steiner Verlag, Dornach, Switzerland) presently runs to 354 titles, organized either by type of work (written or spoken), chronology, audience (public or other), or subject (education, art, etc.). For ease of comparison, the Collected Works in English [CW] follows the German organization exactly. A complete listing of the CWs follows with literal translations of the German titles. Other than in the case of the books published in his lifetime, titles were rarely given by Rudolf Steiner himself, and were often provided by the editors of the German editions. The titles in English are not necessarily the same as the German; and, indeed, over the past 75 years have frequently been different, with the same book sometimes appearing under different titles.

For ease of identification and to avoid confusion, we suggest that readers looking for a title should do so by CW number. Because the work of creating the Collected Works of Rudolf Steiner is an ongoing process, with new titles being published every year, we have not indicated in this listing which books are presently available. To find out what titles in the Collected Works are currently in print, please check our website at www.rudolfsteinerpress.com (or www.steinerbooks.org for US readers).

Written Work

CW 1 Goethe: Natural-Scientific Writings, Introduction, with Footnotes and Explanations in the text by Rudolf Steiner

CW 2 Outlines of an Epistemology of the Goethean World View, with Special Consideration of Schiller

CW 3 Truth and Science

CW 4 The Philosophy of Freedom

CW 4a Documents to 'The Philosophy of Freedom'

CW 5 Friedrich Nietzsche, A Fighter against His Time

CW 6 Goethe's Worldview
CW 6a Now in CW 30
CW 7 Mysticism at the Dawn of Modern Spiritual Life and Its Relationship with Modern Worldviews
CW 8 Christianity as Mystical Fact and the Mysteries of Antiquity
CW 9 Theosophy: An Introduction into Supersensible World Knowledge and Human Purpose
CW 10 How Does One Attain Knowledge of Higher Worlds?
CW 11 From the Akasha-Chronicle
CW 12 Levels of Higher Knowledge
CW 13 Occult Science in Outline
CW 14 Four Mystery Dramas
CW 15 The Spiritual Guidance of the Individual and Humanity
CW 16 A Way to Human Self-Knowledge: Eight Meditations
CW 17 The Threshold of the Spiritual World. Aphoristic Comments
CW 18 The Riddles of Philosophy in Their History, Presented as an Outline
CW 19 Contained in CW 24
CW 20 The Riddles of the Human Being: Articulated and Unarticulated in the Thinking, Views and Opinions of a Series of German and Austrian Personalities
CW 21 The Riddles of the Soul
CW 22 Goethe's Spiritual Nature and its Revelation in 'Faust' and through the 'Fairy Tale of the Snake and the Lily'
CW 23 The Central Points of the Social Question in the Necessities of Life in the Present and the Future
CW 24 Essays Concerning the Threefold Division of the Social Organism and the Period 1915-1921
CW 25 Cosmology, Religion and Philosophy
CW 26 Anthroposophical Leading Thoughts
CW 27 Fundamentals for Expansion of the Art of Healing according to Spiritual-Scientific Insights
CW28 The Course of My Life
CW 29 Collected Essays on Dramaturgy, 1889-1900
CW 30 Methodical Foundations of Anthroposophy: Collected Essays on Philosophy, Natural Science, Aesthetics and Psychology, 1884-1901
CW 31 Collected Essays on Culture and Current Events, 1887-1901
CW 32 Collected Essays on Literature, 1884-1902
CW 33 Biographies and Biographical Sketches, 1894-1905
CW 34 Lucifer-Gnosis: Foundational Essays on Anthroposophy and Reports from the Periodicals 'Lucifer' and 'Lucifer-Gnosis,' 1903-1908
CW 35 Philosophy and Anthroposophy: Collected Essays, 1904-1923
CW 36 The Goetheanum-Idea in the Middle of the Cultural Crisis of the Present: Collected Essays from the Periodical 'Das Goetheanum,' 1921-1925

CW 37 Now in CWs 260a and 251
CW 38 Letters, Vol. 1: 1881-1890
CW 39 Letters, Vol. 2: 1890-1925
CW 40 Truth-Wrought Words
CW 40a Sayings, Poems and Mantras; Supplementary Volume
CW 42 Now in CWs 264-266
CW 43 Stage Adaptations
CW 44 On the Four Mystery Dramas. Sketches, Fragments and Paralipomena on the Four Mystery Dramas
CW 45 Anthroposophy: A Fragment from the Year 1910

Public Lectures

CW 51 On Philosophy, History and Literature
CW 52 Spiritual Teachings Concerning the Soul and Observation of the World
CW 53 The Origin and Goal of the Human Being
CW 54 The Riddles of the World and Anthroposophy
CW 55 Knowledge of the Supersensible in Our Times and Its Meaning for Life Today
CW 56 Knowledge of the Soul and of the Spirit
CW 57 Where and How Does One Find the Spirit?
CW 58 The Metamorphoses of the Soul Life. Paths of Soul Experiences: Part One
CW 59 The Metamorphoses of the Soul Life. Paths of Soul Experiences: Part Two
CW 60 The Answers of Spiritual Science to the Biggest Questions of Existence
CW 61 Human History in the Light of Spiritual Research
CW 62 Results of Spiritual Research
CW 63 Spiritual Science as a Treasure for Life
CW 64 Out of Destiny-Burdened Times
CW 65 Out of Central European Spiritual Life
CW 66 Spirit and Matter, Life and Death
CW 67 The Eternal in the Human Soul. Immortality and Freedom
CW 68 Public lectures in various cities, 1906-1918
CW 69 Public lectures in various cities, 1906-1918
CW 70 Public lectures in various cities, 1906-1918
CW 71 Public lectures in various cities, 1906-1918
CW 72 Freedom—Immortality—Social Life
CW 73 The Supplementing of the Modern Sciences through Anthroposophy
CW 73a Specialized Fields of Knowledge and Anthroposophy
CW 74 The Philosophy of Thomas Aquinas
CW 75 Public lectures in various cities, 1906-1918
CW 76 The Fructifying Effect of Anthroposophy on Specialized Fields
CW 77a The Task of Anthroposophy in Relation to Science and Life: The Darmstadt College Course
CW 77b Art and Anthroposophy. The Goetheanum-Impulse

CW 78 Anthroposophy, Its Roots of Knowledge and Fruits for Life
CW 79 The Reality of the Higher Worlds
CW 80 Public lectures in various cities, 1922
CW 81 Renewal-Impulses for Culture and Science—Berlin College Course
CW 82 So that the Human Being Can Become a Complete Human Being
CW 83 Western and Eastern World-Contrast. Paths to Understanding It through Anthroposophy
CW 84 What Did the Goetheanum Intend and What Should Anthroposophy Do?

Lectures to the Members of the Anthroposophical Society

CW 88 Concerning the Astral World and Devachan
CW 89 Consciousness—Life—Form. Fundamental Principles of a Spiritual-Scientific Cosmology
CW 90 Participant Notes from the Lectures during the Years 1903-1905
CW 91 Participant Notes from the Lectures during the Years 1903-1905
CW 92 The Occult Truths of Ancient Myths and Sagas
CW 93 The Temple Legend and the Golden Legend
CW 93a Fundamentals of Esotericism
CW 94 Cosmogony. Popular Occultism. The Gospel of John. The Theosophy in the Gospel of John
CW 95 At the Gates of Theosophy
CW 96 Origin-Impulses of Spiritual Science. Christian Esotericism in the Light of New Spirit-Knowledge
CW 97 The Christian Mystery
CW 98 Nature Beings and Spirit Beings—Their Effects in Our Visible World
CW 99 The Theosophy of the Rosicrucians
CW 100 Human Development and Christ-Knowledge
CW 101 Myths and Legends. Occult Signs and Symbols
CW 102 The Working into Human Beings by Spiritual Beings
CW 103 The Gospel of John
CW 104 The Apocalypse of John
CW 104a From the Picture-Script of the Apocalypse of John
CW 105 Universe, Earth, the Human Being: Their Being and Development, as well as Their Reflection in the Connection between Egyptian Mythology and Modern Culture
CW 106 Egyptian Myths and Mysteries in Relation to the Active Spiritual Forces of the Present
CW 107 Spiritual-Scientific Knowledge of the Human Being
CW 108 Answering the Questions of Life and the World through Anthroposophy
CW 109 The Principle of Spiritual Economy in Connection with the Question of Reincarnation. An Aspect of the Spiritual Guidance of Humanity
CW 110 The Spiritual Hierarchies and Their Reflection in the Physical World. Zodiac, Planets and Cosmos

CW 111 Contained in CW 109
CW 112 The Gospel of John in Relation to the Three Other Gospels, Especially the Gospel of Luke
CW 113 The Orient in the Light of the Occident. The Children of Lucifer and the Brothers of Christ
CW 114 The Gospel of Luke
CW 115 Anthroposophy—Psychosophy—Pneumatosophy
CW 116 The Christ-Impulse and the Development of I-Consciousness
CW 117 The Deeper Secrets of the Development of Humanity in Light of the Gospels
CW 118 The Event of the Christ-Appearance in the Etheric World
CW 119 Macrocosm and Microcosm. The Large World and the Small World. Soul-Questions, Life-Questions, Spirit-Questions
CW 120 The Revelation of Karma
CW 121 The Mission of Individual Folk-Souls in Connection with Germanic-Nordic Mythology
CW 122 The Secrets of the Biblical Creation-Story. The Six-Day Work in the First Book of Moses
CW 123 The Gospel of Matthew
CW 124 Excursus in the Area of the Gospel of Mark
CW 125 Paths and Goals of the Spiritual Human Being. Life Questions in the Light of Spiritual Science
CW 126 Occult History. Esoteric Observations of the Karmic Relationships of Personalities and Events of World History
CW 127 The Mission of the New Spiritual Revelation. The Christ-Event as the Middle-Point of Earth Evolution
CW 128 An Occult Physiology
CW 129 Wonders of the World, Trials of the Soul, and Revelations of the Spirit
CW 130 Esoteric Christianity and the Spiritual Guidance of Humanity
CW 131 From Jesus to Christ
CW 132 Evolution from the View Point of the Truth
CW 133 The Earthly and the Cosmic Human Being
CW 134 The World of the Senses and the World of the Spirit
CW 135 Reincarnation and Karma and their Meaning for the Culture of the Present
CW 136 The Spiritual Beings in Celestial Bodies and the Realms of Nature
CW 137 The Human Being in the Light of Occultism, Theosophy and Philosophy
CW 138 On Initiation. On Eternity and the Passing Moment. On the Light of the Spirit and the Darkness of Life
CW 139 The Gospel of Mark
CW 140 Occult Investigation into the Life between Death and New Birth. The Living Interaction between Life and Death
CW 141 Life between Death and New Birth in Relationship to Cosmic Facts

CW 142 The Bhagavad Gita and the Letters of Paul
CW 143 Experiences of the Supersensible. Three Paths of the Soul to Christ
CW 144 The Mysteries of the East and of Christianity
CW 145 What Significance Does Occult Development of the Human Being Have for the Sheaths—Physical Body, Etheric Body, Astral Body, and Self?
CW 146 The Occult Foundations of the Bhagavad Gita
CW 147 The Secrets of the Threshold
CW 148 Out of Research in the Akasha: The Fifth Gospel
CW 149 Christ and the Spiritual World. Concerning the Search for the Holy Grail
CW 150 The World of the Spirit and Its Extension into Physical Existence; The Influence of the Dead in the World of the Living
CW 151 Human Thought and Cosmic Thought
CW 152 Preliminary Stages to the Mystery of Golgotha
CW 153 The Inner Being of the Human Being and Life Between Death and New Birth
CW 154 How Does One Gain an Understanding of the Spiritual World? The Flowing in of Spiritual Impulses from out of the World of the Deceased
CW 155 Christ and the Human Soul. Concerning the Meaning of Life. Theosophical Morality. Anthroposophy and Christianity
CW 156 Occult Reading and Occult Hearing
CW 157 Human Destinies and the Destiny of Peoples
CW 157a The Formation of Destiny and the Life after Death
CW 158 The Connection Between the Human Being and the Elemental World. Kalevala—Olaf Åsteson—The Russian People—The World as the Result of the Influences of Equilibrium
CW 159 The Mystery of Death. The Nature and Significance of Middle Europe and the European Folk Spirits
CW 160 In CW 159
CW 161 Paths of Spiritual Knowledge and the Renewal of the Artistic Worldview
CW 162 Questions of Art and Life in Light of Spiritual Science
CW 163 Coincidence, Necessity and Providence. Imaginative Knowledge and the Processes after Death
CW 164 The Value of Thinking for a Knowledge That Satisfies the Human Being. The Relationship of Spiritual Science to Natural Science
CW 165 The Spiritual Unification of Humanity through the Christ-Impulse
CW 166 Necessity and Freedom in the Events of the World and in Human Action
CW 167 The Present and the Past in the Human Spirit
CW 168 The Connection between the Living and the Dead
CW 169 World-being and Selfhood
CW 170 The Riddle of the Human Being. The Spiritual Background of Human History. Cosmic and Human History, Vol. 1

CW 171 Inner Development-Impulses of Humanity. Goethe and the Crisis of the 19th Century. Cosmic and Human History, Vol. 2
CW 172 The Karma of the Vocation of the Human Being in Connection with Goethe's Life. Cosmic and Human History, Vol. 3
CW 173 Contemporary-Historical Considerations: The Karma of Untruthfulness, Part One. Cosmic and Human History, Vol. 4
CW 174 Contemporary-Historical Considerations: The Karma of Untruthfulness, Part Two. Cosmic and Human History, Vol. 5
CW 174a Middle Europe between East and West. Cosmic and Human History, Vol. 6
CW 174b The Spiritual Background of the First World War. Cosmic and Human History, Vol. 7
CW 175 Building Stones for an Understanding of the Mystery of Golgotha. Cosmic and Human Metamorphoses
CW 176 Truths of Evolution of the Individual and Humanity. The Karma of Materialism
CW 177 The Spiritual Background of the Outer World. The Fall of the Spirits of Darkness. Spiritual Beings and Their Effects, Vol. 1
CW 178 Individual Spiritual Beings and their Influence in the Soul of the Human Being. Spiritual Beings and their Effects, Vol. 2
CW 179 Spiritual Beings and Their Effects. Historical Necessity and Freedom. The Influences on Destiny from out of the World of the Dead. Spiritual Beings and Their Effects, Vol. 3
CW 180 Mystery Truths and Christmas Impulses. Ancient Myths and their Meaning. Spiritual Beings and Their Effects, Vol. 4
CW 181 Earthly Death and Cosmic Life. Anthroposophical Gifts for Life. Necessities of Consciousness for the Present and the Future.
CW 182 Death as Transformation of Life
CW 183 The Science of the Development of the Human Being
CW 184 The Polarity of Duration and Development in Human Life. The Cosmic Pre-History of Humanity
CW 185 Historical Symptomology
CW 185a Historical-Developmental Foundations for Forming a Social Judgement
CW 186 The Fundamental Social Demands of Our Time—In Changed Situations
CW 187 How Can Humanity Find the Christ Again? The Threefold Shadow-Existence of our Time and the New Christ-Light
CW 188 Goetheanism, a Transformation-Impulse and Resurrection-Thought. Science of the Human Being and Science of Sociology
CW 189 The Social Question as a Question of Consciousness. The Spiritual Background of the Social Question, Vol. 1
CW 190 Impulses of the Past and the Future in Social Occurrences. The Spiritual Background of the Social Question, Vol. 2

CW 191 Social Understanding from Spiritual-Scientific Cognition. The Spiritual Background of the Social Question, Vol. 3
CW 192 Spiritual-Scientific Treatment of Social and Pedagogical Questions
CW 193 The Inner Aspect of the Social Riddle. Luciferic Past and Ahrimanic Future
CW 194 The Mission of Michael. The Revelation of the Actual Mysteries of the Human Being
CW 195 Cosmic New Year and the New Year Idea
CW 196 Spiritual and Social Transformations in the Development of Humanity
CW 197 Polarities in the Development of Humanity: West and East Materialism and Mysticism Knowledge and Belief
CW 198 Healing Factors for the Social Organism
CW 199 Spiritual Science as Knowledge of the Foundational Impulses of Social Formation
CW 200 The New Spirituality and the Christ-Experience of the 20th Century
CW 201 The Correspondences Between Microcosm and Macrocosm. The Human Being—A Hieroglyph of the Universe. The Human Being in Relationship with the Cosmos: 1
CW 202 The Bridge between the World-Spirituality and the Physical Aspect of the Human Being. The Search for the New Isis, the Divine Sophia. The Human Being in Relationship with the Cosmos: 2
CW 203 The Responsibility of Human Beings for the Development of the World through their Spiritual Connection with the Planet Earth and the World of the Stars. The Human Being in Relationship with the Cosmos: 3
CW 204 Perspectives of the Development of Humanity. The Materialistic Knowledge-Impulse and the Task of Anthroposophy. The Human Being in Relationship with the Cosmos: 4
CW 205 Human Development, World-Soul, and World-Spirit. Part One: The Human Being as a Being of Body and Soul in Relationship to the World. The Human Being in Relationship with the Cosmos: 5
CW 206 Human Development, World-Soul, and World-Spirit. Part Two: The Human Being as a Spiritual Being in the Process of Historical Development. The Human Being in Relationship with the Cosmos: 6
CW 207 Anthroposophy as Cosmosophy. Part One: Characteristic Features of the Human Being in the Earthly and the Cosmic Realms. The Human Being in Relationship with the Cosmos: 7
CW 208 Anthroposophy as Cosmosophy. Part Two: The Forming of the Human Being as the Result of Cosmic Influence. The Human Being in Relationship with the Cosmos: 8
CW 209 Nordic and Central European Spiritual Impulses. The Festival of the Appearance of Christ. The Human Being in Relationship with the Cosmos: 9

CW 210 Old and New Methods of Initiation. Drama and Poetry in the Change of Consciousness in the Modern Age
CW 211 The Sun Mystery and the Mystery of Death and Resurrection. Exoteric and Esoteric Christianity
CW 212 Human Soul Life and Spiritual Striving in Connection with World and Earth Development
CW 213 Human Questions and World Answers
CW 214 The Mystery of the Trinity: The Human Being in Relationship with the Spiritual World in the Course of Time
CW 215 Philosophy, Cosmology, and Religion in Anthroposophy
CW 216 The Fundamental Impulses of the World-Historical Development of Humanity
CW 217 Spiritually Active Forces in the Coexistence of the Older and Younger Generations. Pedagogical Course for Youth
CW 217a Youth's Cognitive Task
CW 218 Spiritual Connections in the Forming of the Human Organism
CW 219 The Relationship of the World of the Stars to the Human Being, and of the Human Being to the World of the Stars. The Spiritual Communion of Humanity
CW 220 Living Knowledge of Nature. Intellectual Fall and Spiritual Redemption
CW 221 Earth-Knowing and Heaven-Insight
CW 222 The Imparting of Impulses to World-Historical Events through Spiritual Powers
CW 223 The Cycle of the Year as Breathing Process of the Earth and the Four Great Festival-Seasons. Anthroposophy and the Human Heart (*Gemüt*)
CW 224 The Human Soul and its Connection with Divine-Spiritual Individualities. The Internalization of the Festivals of the Year
CW 225 Three Perspectives of Anthroposophy. Cultural Phenomena observed from a Spiritual-Scientific Perspective
CW 226 Human Being, Human Destiny, and World Development
CW 227 Initiation-Knowledge
CW 228 Science of Initiation and Knowledge of the Stars. The Human Being in the Past, the Present, and the Future from the Viewpoint of the Development of Consciousness
CW 229 The Experiencing of the Course of the Year in Four Cosmic Imaginations
CW 230 The Human Being as Harmony of the Creative, Building, and Formative World-Word
CW 231 The Supersensible Human Being, Understood Anthroposophically
CW 232 The Forming of the Mysteries
CW 233 World History Illuminated by Anthroposophy and as the Foundation for Knowledge of the Human Spirit

CW 233a Mystery Sites of the Middle Ages: Rosicrucianism and the Modern Initiation-Principle. The Festival of Easter as Part of the History of the Mysteries of Humanity
CW 234 Anthroposophy. A Summary after 21 Years
CW 235 Esoteric Observations of Karmic Relationships in 6 Volumes, Vol. 1
CW 236 Esoteric Observations of Karmic Relationships in 6 Volumes, Vol. 2
CW 237 Esoteric Observations of Karmic Relationships in 6 Volumes, Vol. 3: The Karmic Relationships of the Anthroposophical Movement
CW 238 Esoteric Observations of Karmic Relationships in 6 Volumes, Vol. 4: The Spiritual Life of the Present in Relationship to the Anthroposophical Movement
CW 239 Esoteric Observations of Karmic Relationships in 6 Volumes, Vol. 5
CW 240 Esoteric Observations of Karmic Relationships in 6 Volumes, Vol. 6
CW 243 The Consciousness of the Initiate
CW 245 Instructions for an Esoteric Schooling
CW 250 The Building-Up of the Anthroposophical Society. From the Beginning to the Outbreak of the First World War
CW 251 The History of the Goetheanum Building-Association
CW 252 Life in the Anthroposophical Society from the First World War to the Burning of the First Goetheanum
CW 253 The Problems of Living Together in the Anthroposophical Society. On the Dornach Crisis of 1915. With Highlights on Swedenborg's Clairvoyance, the Views of Freudian Psychoanalysts, and the Concept of Love in Relation to Mysticism
CW 254 The Occult Movement in the 19th Century and Its Relationship to World Culture. Significant Points from the Exoteric Cultural Life around the Middle of the 19th Century
CW 255 Rudolf Steiner during the First World War
CW 255a Anthroposophy and the Reformation of Society. On the History of the Threefold Movement
CW 255b Anthroposophy and Its Opponents, 1919–1921
CW 256 How Can the Anthroposophical Movement Be Financed?
CW 256a Futurum, Inc. / International Laboratories, Inc.
CW 256b The Coming Day, Inc.
CW 257 Anthroposophical Community-Building
CW 258 The History of and Conditions for the Anthroposophical Movement in Relationship to the Anthroposophical Society. A Stimulus to Self-Contemplation
CW 259 The Year of Destiny 1923 in the History of the Anthroposophical Society. From the Burning of the Goetheanum to the Christmas Conference
CW 260 The Christmas Conference for the Founding of the General Anthroposophical Society

CW 260a The Constitution of the General Anthroposophical Society and the School for Spiritual Science. The Rebuilding of the Goetheanum
CW 261 Our Dead. Addresses, Words of Remembrance, and Meditative Verses, 1906-1924
CW 262 Rudolf Steiner and Marie Steiner-von Sivers: Correspondence and Documents, 1901-1925
CW 263/1 Rudolf Steiner and Edith Maryon: Correspondence: Letters, Verses, Sketches, 1912-1924
CW 264 On the History and the Contents of the First Section of the Esoteric School from 1904 to 1914. Letters, Newsletters, Documents, Lectures
CW 265 On the History and from the Contents of the Ritual-Knowledge Section of the Esoteric School from 1904 to 1914. Documents, and Lectures from the Years 1906 to 1914, as well as on New Approaches to Ritual-Knowledge Work in the Years 1921–1924
CW 266/1 From the Contents of the Esoteric Lessons. Volume 1: 1904–1909. Notes from Memory of Participants. Meditation texts from the notes of Rudolf Steiner
CW 266/2 From the Contents of the Esoteric Lessons. Volume 2: 1910–1912. Notes from Memory of Participants
CW 266/3 From the Contents of the Esoteric Lessons. Volume 3: 1913, 1914 and 1920–1923. Notes from Memory of Participants. Meditation texts from the notes of Rudolf Steiner
CW 267 Soul-Exercises: Vol. 1: Exercises with Word and Image Meditations for the Methodological Development of Higher Powers of Knowledge, 1904–1924
CW 268 Soul-Exercises: Vol. 2: Mantric Verses, 1903–1925
CW 269 Ritual Texts for the Celebration of the Free Christian Religious Instruction. The Collected Verses for Teachers and Students of the Waldorf School
CW 270 Esoteric Instructions for the First Class of the School for Spiritual Science at the Goetheanum 1924, 4 Volumes
CW 271 Art and Knowledge of Art. Foundations of a New Aesthetic
CW 272 Spiritual-Scientific Commentary on Goethe's 'Faust' in Two Volumes. Vol. 1: Faust, the Striving Human Being
CW 273 Spiritual-Scientific Commentary on Goethe's 'Faust' in Two Volumes. Vol. 2: The Faust-Problem
CW 274 Addresses for the Christmas Plays from the Old Folk Traditions
CW 275 Art in the Light of Mystery-Wisdom
CW 276 The Artistic in Its Mission in the World. The Genius of Language. The World of Self-Revealing Radiant Appearances—Anthroposophy and Art. Anthroposophy and Poetry
CW 277 Eurythmy. The Revelation of the Speaking Soul
CW 277a The Origin and Development of Eurythmy

CW 278	Eurythmy as Visible Song
CW 279	Eurythmy as Visible Speech
CW 280	The Method and Nature of Speech Formation
CW 281	The Art of Recitation and Declamation
CW 282	Speech Formation and Dramatic Art
CW 283	The Nature of Things Musical and the Experience of Tone in the Human Being
CW 284/285	Images of Occult Seals and Pillars. The Munich Congress of Whitsun 1907 and Its Consequences
CW 286	Paths to a New Style of Architecture. 'And the Building Becomes Human'
CW 287	The Building at Dornach as a Symbol of Historical Becoming and an Artistic Transformation Impulse
CW 288	Style-Forms in the Living Organic
CW 289	The Building-Idea of the Goetheanum: Lectures with Slides from the Years 1920–1921
CW 290	The Building-Idea of the Goetheanum: Lectures with Slides from the Years 1920–1921
CW 291	The Nature of Colours
CW 291a	Knowledge of Colours. Supplementary Volume to 'The Nature of Colours'
CW 292	Art History as Image of Inner Spiritual Impulses
CW 293	General Knowledge of the Human Being as the Foundation of Pedagogy
CW 294	The Art of Education, Methodology and Didactics
CW 295	The Art of Education: Seminar Discussions and Lectures on Lesson Planning
CW 296	The Question of Education as a Social Question
CW 297	The Idea and Practice of the Waldorf School
CW 297a	Education for Life: Self-Education and the Practice of Pedagogy
CW 298	Rudolf Steiner in the Waldorf School
CW 299	Spiritual-Scientific Observations on Speech
CW 300a	Conferences with the Teachers of the Free Waldorf School in Stuttgart, 1919 to 1924, in 3 Volumes, Vol. 1
CW 300b	Conferences with the Teachers of the Free Waldorf School in Stuttgart, 1919 to 1924, in 3 Volumes, Vol. 2
CW 300c	Conferences with the Teachers of the Free Waldorf School in Stuttgart, 1919 to 1924, in 3 Volumes, Vol. 3
CW 301	The Renewal of Pedagogical-Didactical Art through Spiritual Science
CW 302	Knowledge of the Human Being and the Forming of Class Lessons
CW 302a	Education and Teaching from a Knowledge of the Human Being
CW 303	The Healthy Development of the Human Being
CW 304	Methods of Education and Teaching Based on Anthroposophy
CW 304a	Anthroposophical Knowledge of the Human Being and Pedagogy

CW 305 The Soul-Spiritual Foundational Forces of the Art of Education. Spiritual Values in Education and Social Life
CW 306 Pedagogical Praxis from the Viewpoint of a Spiritual-Scientific Knowledge of the Human Being. The Education of the Child and Young Human Beings
CW 307 The Spiritual Life of the Present and Education
CW 308 The Method of Teaching and the Life-Requirements for Teaching
CW 309 Anthroposophical Pedagogy and Its Prerequisites
CW 310 The Pedagogical Value of a Knowledge of the Human Being and the Cultural Value of Pedagogy
CW 311 The Art of Education from an Understanding of the Being of Humanity
CW 312 Spiritual Science and Medicine
CW 313 Spiritual-Scientific Viewpoints on Therapy
CW 314 Physiology and Therapy Based on Spiritual Science
CW 315 Curative Eurythmy
CW 316 Meditative Observations and Instructions for a Deepening of the Art of Healing
CW 317 The Curative Education Course
CW 318 The Working Together of Doctors and Pastors
CW 319 Anthroposophical Knowledge of the Human Being and Medicine
CW 320 Spiritual-Scientific Impulses for the Development of Physics 1: The First Natural-Scientific Course: Light, Colour, Tone, Mass, Electricity, Magnetism
CW 321 Spiritual-Scientific Impulses for the Development of Physics 2: The Second Natural-Scientific Course: Warmth at the Border of Positive and Negative Materiality
CW 322 The Borders of the Knowledge of Nature
CW 323 The Relationship of the various Natural-Scientific Fields to Astronomy
CW 324 Nature Observation, Mathematics, and Scientific Experimentation and Results from the Viewpoint of Anthroposophy
CW 324a The Fourth Dimension in Mathematics and Reality
CW 325 Natural Science and the World-Historical Development of Humanity since Ancient Times
CW 326 The Moment of the Coming Into Being of Natural Science in World History and Its Development Since Then
CW 327 Spiritual-Scientific Foundations for Success in Farming. The Agricultural Course
CW 328 The Social Question
CW 329 The Liberation of the Human Being as the Foundation for a New Social Form
CW 330 The Renewal of the Social Organism
CW 331 Work-Council and Socialization
CW 332 The Alliance for Threefolding and the Total Reform of Society. The Council on Culture and the Liberation of the Spiritual Life

CW 332a The Social Future
CW 333 Freedom of Thought and Social Forces
CW 334 From the Unified State to the Threefold Social Organism
CW 335 The Crisis of the Present and the Path to Healthy Thinking
CW 336 The Great Questions of the Times and Anthroposophical Spiritual Knowledge
CW 337a Social Ideas, Social Reality, Social Practice, Vol. 1: Question-and-Answer Evenings and Study Evenings of the Alliance for the Threefold Social Organism in Stuttgart, 1919-1920
CW 337b Social Ideas, Social Realities, Social Practice, Vol. 2: Discussion Evenings of the Swiss Alliance for the Threefold Social Organism
CW 338 How Does One Work on Behalf of the Impulse for the Threefold Social Organism?
CW 339 Anthroposophy, Threefold Social Organism, and the Art of Public Speaking
CW 340 The National-Economics Course. The Tasks of a New Science of Economics, Volume 1
CW 341 The National-Economics Seminar. The Tasks of a New Science of Economics, Volume 2
CW 342 Lectures and Courses on Christian Religious Work, Vol. 1: Anthroposophical Foundations for a Renewed Christian Religious Working
CW 343 Lectures and Courses on Christian Religious Work, Vol. 2: Spiritual Knowledge—Religious Feeling—Cultic Doing
CW 344 Lectures and Courses on Christian Religious Work, Vol. 3: Lectures at the Founding of the Christian Community
CW 345 Lectures and Courses on Christian Religious Work, Vol. 4: Concerning the Nature of the Working Word
CW 346 Lectures and Courses on Christian Religious Work, Vol. 5: The Apocalypse and the Work of the Priest
CW 347 The Knowledge of the Nature of the Human Being According to Body, Soul and Spirit. On Earlier Conditions of the Earth
CW 348 On Health and Illness. Foundations of a Spiritual-Scientific Doctrine of the Senses
CW 349 On the Life of the Human Being and of the Earth. On the Nature of Christianity
CW 350 Rhythms in the Cosmos and in the Human Being. How Does One Come To See the Spiritual World?
CW 351 The Human Being and the World. The Influence of the Spirit in Nature. On the Nature of Bees
CW 352 Nature and the Human Being Observed Spiritual-Scientifically
CW 353 The History of Humanity and the World-Views of the Folk Cultures
CW 354 The Creation of the World and the Human Being. Life on Earth and the Influence of the Stars

SIGNIFICANT EVENTS IN THE LIFE OF RUDOLF STEINER

1829: June 23: birth of Johann Steiner (1829–1910)—Rudolf Steiner's father—in Geras, Lower Austria.

1834: May 8: birth of Franciska Blie (1834–1918)—Rudolf Steiner's mother—in Horn, Lower Austria. 'My father and mother were both children of the glorious Lower Austrian forest district north of the Danube.'

1860: May 16: marriage of Johann Steiner and Franciska Blie.

1861: February 25: birth of *Rudolf Joseph Lorenz Steiner* in Kraljevec, Croatia, near the border with Hungary, where Johann Steiner works as a telegrapher for the South Austria Railroad. Rudolf Steiner is baptized two days later, February 27, the date usually given as his birthday.

1862: Summer: the family moves to Modling, Lower Austria.

1863: The family moves to Pottschach, Lower Austria, near the Styrian border, where Johann Steiner becomes station master. 'The view stretched to the mountains . . . majestic peaks in the distance and the sweet charm of nature in the immediate surroundings.'

1864: November 15: birth of Rudolf Steiner's sister, Leopoldine (d. November 1, 1927). She will become a seamstress and live with her parents for the rest of her life.

1866: July 28: birth of Rudolf Steiner's deaf-mute brother, Gustav (d. May 1, 1941).

1867: Rudolf Steiner enters the village school. Following a disagreement between his father and the schoolmaster, whose wife falsely accused the boy of causing a commotion, Rudolf Steiner is taken out of school and taught at home.

1868: A critical experience. Unknown to the family, an aunt dies in a distant town. Sitting in the station waiting room, Rudolf Steiner sees her 'form,' which speaks to him, asking for help. 'Beginning with this experience, a new soul life began in the boy, one in which not only the outer trees and mountains spoke to him, but also the worlds that lay behind them. From this moment on, the boy began to live with the spirits of nature . . .'

1869: The family moves to the peaceful, rural village of Neudorfl, near Wiener Neustadt in present-day Austria. Rudolf Steiner attends the village school. Because of the 'unorthodoxy' of his writing and spelling, he has to do 'extra lessons'.

1870: Through a book lent to him by his tutor, he discovers geometry: 'To grasp something purely in the spirit brought me inner happiness. I know that I first learned happiness through geometry.' The same tutor allows him to draw, while other students still struggle with their reading and writing. 'An artistic element' thus enters his education.

1871: Though his parents are not religious, Rudolf Steiner becomes a 'church child,' a favourite of the priest, who was 'an exceptional character.' 'Up to the age of ten or eleven, among those I came to know, he was far and away the most significant.' Among other things, he introduces Steiner to Copernican, heliocentric cosmology. As an altar boy, Rudolf Steiner serves at masses, funerals, and Corpus Christi processions. At year's end, after an incident in which he escapes a thrashing, his father forbids him to go to church.

1872: Rudolf Steiner transfers to grammar school in Wiener-Neustadt, a five-mile walk from home, which must be done in all weathers.

1873–75: Through his teachers and on his own, Rudolf Steiner has many wonderful experiences with science and mathematics. Outside school, he teaches himself analytic geometry, trigonometry, differential equations, and calculus.

1876: Rudolf Steiner begins tutoring other students. He learns bookbinding from his father. He also teaches himself stenography.

1877: Rudolf Steiner discovers Kant's *Critique of Pure Reason,* which he reads and rereads. He also discovers and reads von Rotteck's *World History.*

1878: He studies extensively in contemporary psychology and philosophy.

1879: Rudolf Steiner graduates from high school with honours. His father is transferred to Inzersdorf, near Vienna. He uses his first visit to Vienna 'to purchase a great number of philosophy books'—Kant, Fichte, Schelling, and Hegel, as well as numerous histories of philosophy. His aim: to find a path from the 'I' to nature.

October 1879–1883: Rudolf Steiner attends the Technical College in Vienna—to study mathematics, chemistry, physics, mineralogy, botany, zoology, biology, geology, and mechanics—with a scholarship. He also attends lectures in history and literature, while avidly reading philosophy on his own. His two favourite professors are Karl Julius Schröer (German language and literature) and Edmund Reitlinger (physics). He also audits lectures by Robert Zimmermann on aesthetics and Franz Brentano on philosophy. During this year he begins his friendship with Moritz Zitter (1861–1921), who will help support him financially when he is in Berlin.

1880: Rudolf Steiner attends lectures on Schiller and Goethe by Karl Julius Schröer, who becomes his mentor. Also 'through a remarkable combination of circumstances,' he meets Felix Koguzki, a 'herb gatherer' and healer, who could 'see deeply into the secrets of nature'. Rudolf Steiner will meet and study with this 'emissary of the Master' throughout his time in Vienna.

1881: January: '... I didn't sleep a wink. I was busy with philosophical problems until about 12:30 a.m. Then, finally, I threw myself down on my couch. All my striving during the previous year had been to research whether the following statement by Schelling was true or not: *Within everyone dwells a secret, marvellous capacity to draw back from the stream of time—out of the self clothed in all that comes to us from outside—into our innermost being and there, in the immutable form of the Eternal, to look into ourselves.* I believe, and I am still quite certain of it, that I discovered this capacity in myself; I had long had an inkling of it. Now the whole of idealist philosophy stood before me in modified form. What's a sleepless night compared to that!'

Rudolf Steiner begins communicating with leading thinkers of the day, who send him books in return, which he reads eagerly.

July: 'I am not one of those who dives into the day like an animal in human form. I pursue a quite specific goal, an idealistic aim—knowledge of the truth! This cannot be done offhandedly. It requires the greatest striving in the world, free of all egotism, and equally of all resignation.'

August: Steiner puts down on paper for the first time thoughts for a 'Philosophy of Freedom.' 'The striving for the absolute: this human yearning is freedom.' He also seeks to outline a 'peasant philosophy,' describing what the worldview of a 'peasant'—one who lives close to the earth and the old ways—really is.

1881–1882: Felix Koguzki, the herb gatherer, reveals himself to be the envoy of another, higher initiatory personality, who instructs Rudolf Steiner to penetrate Fichte's philosophy and to master modern scientific thinking as a preparation for right entry into the spirit. This 'Master' also teaches him the double (evolutionary and involutionary) nature of time.

1882: Through the offices of Karl Julius Schröer, Rudolf Steiner is asked by Joseph Kürschner to edit Goethe's scientific works for the *Deutschen National-Literatur* edition. He writes 'A Possible Critique of Atomistic Concepts' and sends it to Friedrich Theodor Vischer.

1883: Rudolf Steiner completes his college studies and begins work on the Goethe project.

1884: First volume of Goethe's *Scientific Writings* (CW 1) appears (March). He lectures on Goethe and Lessing, and Goethe's approach to science. In July, he enters the household of Ladislaus and Pauline Specht as tutor to the four Specht boys. He will live there until 1890. At this time, he meets Josef Breuer (1842–1925), the co-author with Sigmund Freud of *Studies in Hysteria,* who is the Specht family doctor.

1885: While continuing to edit Goethe's writings, Rudolf Steiner reads deeply in contemporary philosophy (Eduard von Hartmann, Johannes Volkelt, and Richard Wahle, among others).

1886: May: Rudolf Steiner sends Kürschner the manuscript of *Outlines of Goethe's Theory of Knowledge* (CW 2), which appears in October, and which he sends out widely. He also meets the poet Marie Eugenie Delle Grazie and writes 'Nature and Our Ideals' for her. He attends her salon, where he meets many priests, theologians, and philosophers, who will become his friends. Meanwhile, the director of the Goethe Archive in Weimar requests his collaboration with the *Sophien* edition of Goethe's works, particularly the writings on colour.

1887: At the beginning of the year, Rudolf Steiner is very sick. As the year progresses and his health improves, he becomes increasingly 'a man of letters,' lecturing, writing essays, and taking part in Austrian cultural life. In August–September, the second volume of Goethe's *Scientific Writings* appears.

1888: January–July: Rudolf Steiner assumes editorship of the 'German Weekly' *(Deutsche Wochenschrift*). He begins lecturing more intensively, giving, for example, a lecture titled 'Goethe as Father of a New Aesthetics.' He meets and becomes soul friends with Friedrich Eckstein (1861–1939), a vegetarian, philosopher of symbolism, alchemist, and musician, who will introduce him to various spiritual currents (including Theosophy) and with whom he will meditate and interpret esoteric and alchemical texts.

1889: Rudolf Steiner first reads Nietzsche *(Beyond Good and Evil).* He encounters Theosophy again and learns of Madame Blavatsky in the theosophical circle around Marie Lang (1858–1934). Here he also meets well-known figures of Austrian life, as well as esoteric figures like the occultist Franz Hartmann and Karl Leinigen-Billigen (translator of C.G. Harrison's *The Transcendental Universe*). During this period, Steiner first reads A.P. Sinnett's *Esoteric Buddhism* and Mabel Collins's *Light on the Path*. He also begins travelling, visiting Budapest, Weimar, and Berlin (where he meets philosopher Eduard von Hartmann).

1890: Rudolf Steiner finishes Volume 3 of Goethe's scientific writings. He begins his doctoral dissertation, which will become *Truth and Science* (CW 3). He also meets the poet and feminist Rosa Mayreder (1858–1938), with whom he can exchange his most intimate thoughts. In September, Rudolf Steiner moves to Weimar to work in the Goethe-Schiller Archive.

1891: Volume 3 of the Kürschner edition of Goethe appears. Meanwhile, Rudolf Steiner edits Goethe's studies in mineralogy and scientific writings for the *Sophien* edition. He meets Ludwig Laistner of the Cotta Publishing Company, who asks for a book on the basic question of metaphysics. From this will result, ultimately, *The Philosophy of Freedom* (CW 4), which will be published not by Cotta but by Emil Felber. In October, Rudolf Steiner takes the oral exam for a doctorate in philosophy, mathematics, and mechanics at Rostock University, receiving his doctorate on the twenty-sixth. In November, he gives his first lecture on Goethe's 'Fairy Tale' in Vienna.

1892: Rudolf Steiner continues work at the Goethe-Schiller Archive and on his *Philosophy of Freedom. Truth and Science,* his doctoral dissertation, is published. Steiner undertakes to write Introductions to books on Schopenhauer and Jean Paul for Cotta. At year's end, he finds lodging with Anna Eunike, née Schulz (1853–1911), a widow with four daughters and a son. He also develops a friendship with Otto Erich Hartleben (1864–1905) with whom he shares literary interests.

1893: Rudolf Steiner begins his habit of producing many reviews and articles. In March, he gives a lecture titled 'Hypnotism, with Reference to Spiritism.' In September, volume 4 of the Kürschner edition is completed. In November, *The Philosophy of Freedom* appears. This year, too, he meets John Henry Mackay (1864–1933), the anarchist, and Max Stirner, a scholar and biographer.

1894: Rudolf Steiner meets Elisabeth Förster Nietzsche, the philosopher's sister, and begins to read Nietzsche in earnest, beginning with the as yet unpublished *Antichrist.* He also meets Ernst Haeckel (1834–1919). In the fall, he begins to write *Nietzsche, A Fighter against His Time* (CW 5).

1895: May, *Nietzsche, A Fighter against His Time* appears.

1896: January 22: Rudolf Steiner sees Friedrich Nietzsche for the first and only time. Moves between the Nietzsche and the Goethe-Schiller

Archives, where he completes his work before year's end. He falls out with Elisabeth Förster Nietzsche, thus ending his association with the Nietzsche Archive.

1897: Rudolf Steiner finishes the manuscript of *Goethe's Worldview* (CW 6). He moves to Berlin with Anna Eunike and begins editorship of the *Magazin für Literatur.* From now on, Steiner will write countless reviews, literary and philosophical articles, and so on. He begins lecturing at the 'Free Literary Society.' In September, he attends the Zionist Congress in Basel. He sides with Dreyfus in the Dreyfus affair.

1898: Rudolf Steiner is very active as an editor in the political, artistic, and theatrical life of Berlin. He becomes friendly with John Henry Mackay and poet Ludwig Jacobowski (1868–1900). He joins Jacobowski's circle of writers, artists, and scientists—'The Coming Ones' (*Die Kommenden*)—and contributes lectures to the group until 1903. He also lectures at the 'League for College Pedagogy.' He writes an article for Goethe's sesquicentennial, 'Goethe's Secret Revelation,' on the 'Fairy Tale of the Green Snake and the Beautiful Lily.'

1898–99: 'This was a trying time for my soul as I looked at Christianity. . . . I was able to progress only by contemplating, by means of spiritual perception, the evolution of Christianity. . . . Conscious knowledge of real Christianity began to dawn in me around the turn of the century. This seed continued to develop. My soul trial occurred shortly before the beginning of the twentieth century. It was decisive for my soul's development that I stood spiritually before the Mystery of Golgotha in a deep and solemn celebration of knowledge.'

1899: Rudolf Steiner begins teaching and giving lectures and lecture cycles at the Workers' College, founded by Wilhelm Liebknecht (1826–1900). He will continue to do so until 1904. Writes: *Literature and Spiritual Life in the Nineteenth Century; Individualism in Philosophy; Haeckel and His Opponents; Poetry in the Present;* and begins what will become (fifteen years later) *The Riddles of Philosophy* (CW 18). He also meets many artists and writers, including Käthe Kollwitz, Stefan Zweig, and Rainer Maria Rilke. On October 31, he marries Anna Eunike.

1900: 'I thought that the turn of the century must bring humanity a new light. It seemed to me that the separation of human thinking and willing from the spirit had peaked. A turn or reversal of direction in human evolution seemed to me a necessity.' Rudolf Steiner finishes *World and Life Views in the Nineteenth Century* (the second part of what will become *The Riddles of Philosophy*) and dedicates it to

Ernst Haeckel. It is published in March. He continues lecturing at *Die Kommenden,* whose leadership he assumes after the death of Jacobowski. Also, he gives the Gutenberg Jubilee lecture before 7,000 typesetters and printers. In September, Rudolf Steiner is invited by Count and Countess Brockdorff to lecture in the Theosophical Library. His first lecture is on Nietzsche. His second lecture is titled 'Goethe's Secret Revelation.' October 6, he begins a lecture cycle on the mystics that will become *Mystics after Modernism* (CW 7). November–December: 'Marie von Sivers appears in the audience. . . .' Also in November, Steiner gives his first lecture at the Giordano Bruno Bund (where he will continue to lecture until May, 1905). He speaks on Bruno and modern Rome, focusing on the importance of the philosophy of Thomas Aquinas as monism.

1901: In continual financial straits, Rudolf Steiner's early friends Moritz Zitter and Rosa Mayreder help support him. In October, he begins the lecture cycle *Christianity as Mystical Fact* (CW 8) at the Theosophical Library. In November, he gives his first 'theosophical lecture' on Goethe's 'Fairy Tale' in Hamburg at the invitation of Wilhelm Hubbe-Schleiden. He also attends a gathering to celebrate the founding of the Theosophical Society at Count and Countess Brockdorff's. He gives a lecture cycle, 'From Buddha to Christ,' for the circle of the *Kommenden.* November 17, Marie von Sivers asks Rudolf Steiner if Theosophy needs a Western–Christian spiritual movement (to complement Theosophy's Eastern emphasis). 'The question was posed. Now, following spiritual laws, I could begin to give an answer. . . .' In December, Rudolf Steiner writes his first article for a theosophical publication. At year's end, the Brockdorffs and possibly Wilhelm Hubbe-Schleiden ask Rudolf Steiner to join the Theosophical Society and undertake the leadership of the German section. Rudolf Steiner agrees, on the condition that Marie von Sivers (then in Italy) work with him.

1902: Beginning in January, Rudolf Steiner attends the opening of the Workers' School in Spandau with Rosa Luxemberg (1870–1919). January 17, Rudolf Steiner joins the Theosophical Society. In April, he is asked to become general secretary of the German Section of the theosophical Society, and works on preparations for its founding. In July, he visits London for a theosophical congress. He meets Bertram Keightly, G.R.S. Mead, A.P. Sinnett, and Annie Besant, among others. In September, *Christianity as Mystical Fact* appears. In October, Rudolf Steiner gives his first public lecture on Theosophy ('Monism and Theosophy') to about three hundred people at the Giordano Bruno Bund. On October 19–21, the

German Section of the Theosophical Society has its first meeting; Rudolf Steiner is the general secretary, and Annie Besant attends. Steiner lectures on practical karma studies. On October 23, Annie Besant inducts Rudolf Steiner into the Esoteric School of the Theosophical Society. On October 25, Steiner begins a weekly series of lectures: 'The Field of Theosophy.' During this year, Rudolf Steiner also first meets Ita Wegman (1876–1943), who will become his close collaborator in his final years.

1903: Rudolf Steiner holds about 300 lectures and seminars. In May, the first issue of the periodical *Luzifer* appears. In June, Rudolf Steiner visits London for the first meeting of the Federation of the European Sections of the Theosophical Society, where he meets Colonel Olcott. He begins to write *Theosophy* (CW 9).

1904: Rudolf Steiner continues lecturing at the Workers' College and elsewhere (about 90 lectures), while lecturing intensively all over Germany among theosophists (about 140 lectures). In February, he meets Carl Unger (1878–1929), who will become a member of the board of the Anthroposophical Society (1913). In March, he meets Michael Bauer (1871–1929), a Christian mystic, who will also be on the board. In May, *Theosophy* appears, with the dedication: 'To the spirit of Giordano Bruno.' Rudolf Steiner and Marie von Sivers visit London for meetings with Annie Besant. June: Rudolf Steiner and Marie von Sivers attend the meeting of the Federation of European Sections of the Theosophical Society in Amsterdam. In July, Steiner begins the articles in *Luzifer-Gnosis* that will become *How to Know Higher Worlds* (CW 10) and *Cosmic Memory* (CW 11). In September, Annie Besant visits Germany. In December, Steiner lectures on Freemasonry. He mentions the High Grade Masonry derived from John Yarker and represented by Theodore Reuss and Karl Kellner as a blank slate 'into which a good image could be placed'.

1905: This year, Steiner ends his non-theosophical lecturing activity. Supported by Marie von Sivers, his theosophical lecturing—both in public and in the Theosophical Society—increases significantly: 'The German Theosophical Movement is of exceptional importance.' Steiner recommends reading, among others, Fichte, Jacob Boehme, and Angelus Silesius. He begins to introduce Christian themes into Theosophy. He also begins to work with doctors (Felix Peipers and Ludwig Noll). In July, he is in London for the Federation of European Sections, where he attends a lecture by Annie Besant: 'I have seldom seen Mrs Besant speak in so inward and heartfelt a manner... Through Mrs Besant I have found the way to H.P. Blavatsky.' September to October, he gives a course of 31 lectures for a small group of esoteric students. In October, the annual meeting of the German Section of the Theosophical Society, which still remains very small, takes place. Rudolf Steiner reports membership has risen from 121 to 377 members. In November, seeking to establish esoteric 'continuity,' Rudolf Steiner and Marie von Sivers participate in a 'Memphis-Misraim' Masonic ceremony. They pay 45 marks for membership. 'Yesterday, you saw how little remains of former esoteric institutions.' 'We are dealing only with a "framework" . . for the present, nothing lies behind it. The occult powers have completely withdrawn.'

1906: Expansion of theosophical work. Rudolf Steiner gives about 245 lectures, only 44 of which take place in Berlin. Cycles are given in Paris, Leipzig, Stuttgart, and Munich. Esoteric work also intensifies. Rudolf Steiner begins writing *An Outline of Esoteric Science* (CW 13). In January, Rudolf Steiner receives permission (a patent) from the Great Orient of the Scottish A & A Thirty-Three Degree Rite of the Order of the Ancient Freemasons of the Memphis-Misraim Rite to direct a chapter under the name 'Mystica Aeterna.' This will become the 'Cognitive-Ritual Section' (also called 'Misraim Service') of the Esoteric School. (See: *Freemasonry and Ritual Work: The Misraim Service,* CW 265.) During this time, Steiner also meets Albert Schweitzer. In May, he is in Paris, where he visits Édouard Schuré. Many Russians attend his lectures (including Konstantin Balmont, Dimitri Mereszkovski, Zinaida Hippius, and Maximilian Woloshin). He attends the General Meeting of the European Federation of the Theosophical Society, at which Col. Olcott is present for the last time. He spends the year's end in Venice and Rome, where he writes and works on his translation of H.P. Blavatsky's *Key to Theosophy.*

1907: Further expansion of the German Theosophical Movement according to the Rosicrucian directive to 'introduce spirit into the world'—in education, in social questions, in art, and in science. In February, Col. Olcott dies in Adyar. Before he dies, Olcott indicates that 'the Masters' wish Annie Besant to succeed him: much politicking ensues. Rudolf Steiner supports Besant's candidacy. April–May: preparations for the Congress of the Federation of European Sections of the Theosophical Society—the great, watershed Whitsun 'Munich Congress,' attended by Annie Besant and others. Steiner decides to separate Eastern and Western (Christian–Rosicrucian) esoteric schools. He takes his esoteric school out of the Theosophical Society (Besant and Rudolf Steiner are 'in harmony' on this). Steiner makes his first lecture tours to Austria and Hungary. That summer, he is in Italy. In September, he visits Édouard Schuré, who will write the Introduction to the French edition of *Christianity as Mystical Fact* in Barr, Alsace. Rudolf Steiner writes the autobiographical statement known as the 'Barr Document.' In *Luzifer-Gnosis*, 'The Education of the Child' appears.

1908: The movement grows (membership: 1,150). Lecturing expands. Steiner makes his first extended lecture tour to Holland and Scandinavia, as well as visits to Naples and Sicily. Themes: St John's Gospel, the Apocalypse, Egypt, science, philosophy, and logic. *Luzifer-Gnosis* ceases publication. In Berlin, Marie von Sivers (with Johanna Mücke (1864–1949) forms the *Philosophisch-Theosophisch* (after 1915 *Philosophisch-Anthroposophisch) Verlag* to publish Steiner's work. Steiner gives lecture cycles titled *The Gospel of St John* (CW 103) and *The Apocalypse* (104).

1909: *An Outline of Esoteric Science* appears. Lecturing and travel continues. Rudolf Steiner's spiritual research expands to include the polarity of Lucifer and Ahriman; the work of great individualities in history; the Maitreya Buddha and the Bodhisattvas; spiritual economy (CW 109); the work of the spiritual hierarchies in heaven and on earth (CW 110). He also deepens and intensifies his research into the Gospels, giving lectures on the Gospel of St Luke (CW 114) with the first mention of two Jesus children. Meets and becomes friends with Christian Morgenstern (1871–1914). In April, he lays the foundation stone for the Malsch model—the building that will lead to the first Goetheanum. In May, the International Congress of the Federation of European Sections of the Theosophical Society takes place in Budapest. Rudolf Steiner receives the Subba Row medal for *How to Know Higher Worlds*. During this time, Charles W. Leadbeater discovers Jiddu Krishnamurti (1895–1986) and proclaims him the future 'world teacher,' the bearer of the Maitreya Buddha and the 'reappearing Christ.' In October, Steiner delivers seminal lectures on 'anthroposophy,' which he will try, unsuccessfully, to rework over the next years into the unfinished work, *Anthroposophy (A Fragment)* (CW 45).

1910: New themes: *The Reappearance of Christ in the Etheric* (CW 118); *The Fifth Gospel; The Mission of Folk Souls* (CW 121); *Occult History* (CW 126); the evolving development of etheric cognitive capacities. Rudolf Steiner continues his Gospel research with *The Gospel of St Matthew* (CW 123). In January, his father dies. In April, he takes a month-long trip to Italy, including Rome, Monte Cassino, and Sicily. He also visits Scandinavia again. July–August, he writes the first Mystery Drama, *The Portal of Initiation* (CW 14). In November, he gives 'psychosophy' lectures. In December, he submits 'On the

Psychological Foundations and Epistemological Framework of Theosophy' to the International Philosophical Congress in Bologna.

1911: The crisis in the Theosophical Society deepens. In January, 'The Order of the Rising Sun,' which will soon become 'The Order of the Star in the East,' is founded for the coming world teacher, Krishnamurti. At the same time, Marie von Sivers, Rudolf Steiner's co-worker, falls ill. Fewer lectures are given, but important new ground is broken. In Prague, in March, Steiner meets Franz Kafka (1883–1924) and Hugo Bergmann (1883–1975). In April, he delivers his paper to the Philosophical Congress. He writes the second Mystery Drama, *The Soul's Probation* (CW 14). Also, while Marie von Sivers is convalescing, Rudolf Steiner begins work on *Calendar 1912/1913*, which will contain the 'Calendar of the Soul' meditations. On March 19, Anna (Eunike) Steiner dies. In September, Rudolf Steiner visits Einsiedeln, birthplace of Paracelsus. In December, Friedrich Rittelmeyer, future founder of the Christian Community, meets Rudolf Steiner. The *Johannes-Bauverein*, the 'building committee,' which would lead to the first Goetheanum (first planned for Munich), is also founded, and a preliminary committee for the founding of an independent association is created that, in the following year, will become the Anthroposophical Society. Important lecture cycles include *Occult Physiology* (CW 128); *Wonders of the World* (CW 129); *From Jesus to Christ* (CW 131). Other themes: esoteric Christianity; Christian Rosenkreutz; the spiritual guidance of humanity; the sense world and the world of the spirit.

1912: Despite the ongoing, now increasing crisis in the Theosophical Society, much is accomplished: *Calendar 1912/1913* is published; eurythmy is created; both the third Mystery Drama, *The Guardian of the Threshold* (CW 14) and *A Way of Self-Knowledge* (CW 16) are written. New (or renewed) themes included life between death and rebirth and karma and reincarnation. Other lecture cycles: *Spiritual Beings in the Heavenly Bodies and in the Kingdoms of Nature* (CW 136); *The Human Being in the Light of Occultism, Theosophy, and Philosophy* (CW 137); *The Gospel of St Mark* (CW 139); and *The Bhagavad Gita and the Epistles of Paul* (CW 142). On May 8, Rudolf Steiner celebrates White Lotus Day, H.P. Blavatsky's death day, which he had faithfully observed for the past decade, for the last time. In August, Rudolf Steiner suggests the 'independent association' be called the 'Anthroposophical Society.' In September, the first eurythmy course takes place. In October, Rudolf Steiner declines recognition of a Theosophical Society lodge dedicated to the Star of the East and decides to expel all Theosophical Society members belonging to the order.

Also, with Marie von Sivers, he first visits Dornach, near Basel, Switzerland, and they stand on the hill where the Goetheanum will be built. In November, a Theosophical Society lodge is opened by direct mandate from Adyar (Annie Besant). In December, a meeting of the German section occurs at which it is decided that belonging to the Order of the Star of the East is incompatible with membership in the Theosophical Society. December 28: informal founding of the Anthroposophical Society in Berlin.

1913: Expulsion of the German section from the Theosophical Society. February 2–3: Foundation meeting of the Anthroposophical Society. Board members include: Marie von Sivers, Michael Bauer, and Carl Unger. September 20: Laying of the foundation stone for the *Johannes Bau* (Goetheanum) in Dornach. Building begins immediately. The fourth Mystery Drama, *The Soul's Awakening* (CW 14), is completed. Also: *The Threshold of the Spiritual World* (CW 147). Lecture cycles include: *The Bhagavad Gita and the Epistles of Paul* and *The Esoteric Meaning of the Bhagavad Gita* (CW 146), which the Russian philosopher Nikolai Berdyaev attends; *The Mysteries of the East and of Christianity* (CW 144); *The Effects of Esoteric Development* (CW 145); and *The Fifth Gospel* (CW 148). In May, Rudolf Steiner is in London and Paris, where anthroposophical work continues.

1914: Building continues on the *Johannes Bau* (Goetheanum) in Dornach, with artists and co-workers from seventeen nations. The general assembly of the Anthroposophical Society takes place. In May, Rudolf Steiner visits Paris, as well as Chartres Cathedral. June 28: assassination in Sarajevo ('Now the catastrophe has happened!'). August 1: War is declared. Rudolf Steiner returns to Germany from Dornach—he will travel back and forth. He writes the last chapter of *The Riddles of Philosophy*. Lecture cycles include: *Human and Cosmic Thought* (CW 151); *Inner Being of Humanity between Death and a New Birth* (CW 153); *Occult Reading and Occult Hearing* (CW 156). December 24: marriage of Rudolf Steiner and Marie von Sivers.

1915: Building continues. Life after death becomes a major theme, also art. Writes: *Thoughts during a Time of War* (CW 24). Lectures include: *The Secret of Death* (CW 159); *The Uniting of Humanity through the Christ Impulse* (CW 165).

1916: Rudolf Steiner begins work with Edith Maryon (1872–1924) on the sculpture 'The Representative of Humanity' ('The Group'—Christ, Lucifer, and Ahriman). He also works with the alchemist Alexander von Bernus on the quarterly *Das Reich*. He writes *The Riddle of Humanity* (CW 20). Lectures include: *Necessity and Freedom in World History and Human Action* (CW 166); *Past and Present in the*

Human Spirit (CW 167); *The Karma of Vocation* (CW 172); *The Karma of Untruthfulness* (CW 173).

1917: Russian Revolution. The U.S. enters the war. Building continues. Rudolf Steiner delineates the idea of the 'threefold nature of the human being' (in a public lecture March 15) and the 'threefold nature of the social organism' (hammered out in May–June with the help of Otto von Lerchenfeld and Ludwig Polzer-Hoditz in the form of two documents titled *Memoranda,* which were distributed in high places). August–September: Rudolf Steiner writes *The Riddles of the Soul* (CW 20). Also: commentary on 'The Chymical Wedding of Christian Rosenkreutz' for Alexander Bernus (Das *Reich*). Lectures include: *The Karma of Materialism* (CW 176); *The Spiritual Background of the Outer World: The Fall of the Spirits of Darkness* (CW 177).

1918: March 18: peace treaty of Brest-Litovsk—'Now everything will truly enter chaos! What is needed is cultural renewal.' June: Rudolf Steiner visits Karlstein (Grail) Castle outside Prague. Lecture cycle: *From Symptom to Reality in Modern History* (CW 185). In mid-November, Emil Molt, of the Waldorf-Astoria Cigarette Company, has the idea of founding a school for his workers' children.

1919: Focus on the threefold social organism: tireless travel, countless lectures, meetings, and publications. At the same time, a new public stage of Anthroposophy emerges as cultural renewal begins. The coming years will see initiatives in pedagogy, medicine, pharmacology, and agriculture. January 27: threefold meeting: 'We must first of all, with the money we have, found free schools that can bring people what they need.' February: first public eurythmy performance in Zurich. Also: 'Appeal to the German People' (CW 24), circulated March 6 as a newspaper insert. In April, *Towards Social Renewal* (CW 23) appears—'perhaps the most widely read of all books on politics appearing since the war'. Rudolf Steiner is asked to undertake the 'direction and leadership' of the school founded by the Waldorf-Astoria Company. Rudolf Steiner begins to talk about the 'renewal' of education. May 30: a building is selected and purchased for the future Waldorf School. August–September, Rudolf Steiner gives a lecture course for Waldorf teachers, *The Foundations of Human Experience (Study of Man)* (CW 293). September 7: Opening of the first Waldorf School. December (into January): first science course, the *Light Course* (CW 320).

1920: The Waldorf School flourishes. New threefold initiatives. Founding of limited companies *Der Kommende Tag* and *Futurum A.G.* to infuse spiritual values into the economic realm. Rudolf Steiner also focuses on the sciences. Lectures: *Introducing Anthroposophical*

Medicine (CW 312); *The Warmth Course* (CW 321); *The Boundaries of Natural Science* (CW 322); *The Redemption of Thinking* (CW 74). February: Johannes Werner Klein—later a co-founder of the Christian Community—asks Rudolf Steiner about the possibility of a 'religious renewal,' a 'Johannine church.' In March, Rudolf Steiner gives the first course for doctors and medical students. In April, a divinity student asks Rudolf Steiner a second time about the possibility of religious renewal. September 27–October 16: anthroposophical 'university course.' December: lectures titled *The Search for the New Isis* (CW 202).

1921: Rudolf Steiner continues his intensive work on cultural renewal, including the uphill battle for the threefold social order. 'University' arts, scientific, theological, and medical courses include: *The Astronomy Course* (CW 323); *Observation, Mathematics, and Scientific Experiment* (CW 324); the *Second Medical Course* (CW 313); *Colour.* In June and September–October, Rudolf Steiner also gives the first two 'priests' courses' (CW 342 and 343). The 'youth movement' gains momentum. Magazines are founded: *Die Drei* (January), and—under the editorship of Albert Steffen (1884–1963)—the weekly, *Das Goetheanum* (August). In February–March, Rudolf Steiner takes his first trip outside Germany since the war (Holland). On April 7, Steiner receives a letter regarding 'religious renewal,' and May 22–23, he agrees to address the question in a practical way. In June, the Klinical-Therapeutic Institute opens in Arlesheim under the direction of Dr Ita Wegman. In August, the Chemical-Pharmaceutical Laboratory opens in Arlesheim (Oskar Schmiedel and Ita Wegman are directors). The Clinical Therapeutic Institute is inaugurated in Stuttgart (Dr Ludwig Noll is director); also the Research Laboratory in Dornach (Ehrenfried Pfeiffer and Gunther Wachsmuth are directors). In November–December, Rudolf Steiner visits Norway.

1922: The first half of the year involves very active public lecturing (thousands attend); in the second half, Rudolf Steiner begins to withdraw and turn toward the Society—'The Society is asleep.' It is 'too weak' to do what is asked of it. The businesses—*Der Kommende Tag* and *Futurum A.G.*—fail. In January, with the help of an agent, Steiner undertakes a twelve-city German lecture tour, accompanied by eurythmy performances. In two weeks he speaks to more than 2,000 people. In April, he gives a 'university course' in The Hague. He also visits England. In June, he is in Vienna for the East–West Congress. In August–September, he is back in England for the Oxford Conference on Education. Returning to Dornach, he gives the lectures *Philosophy, Cosmology, and Religion*

(CW 215), and gives the third priests' course (CW 344). On September 16, The Christian Community is founded. In October–November, Steiner is in Holland and England. He also speaks to the youth: *The Youth Course* (CW 217). In December, Steiner gives lectures titled *The Origins of Natural Science* (CW 326), and *Humanity and the World of Stars: The Spiritual Communion of Humanity* (CW 219). December 31: Fire at the Goetheanum, which is destroyed.

1923: Despite the fire, Rudolf Steiner continues his work unabated. A very hard year. Internal dispersion, dissension, and apathy abound. There is conflict—between old and new visions—within the Society. A wake-up call is needed, and Rudolf Steiner responds with renewed lecturing vitality. His focus: the spiritual context of human life; initiation science; the course of the year; and community building. As a foundation for an artistic school, he creates a series of pastel sketches. Lecture cycles: *The Anthroposophical Movement; Initiation Science* (CW 227) (in Wales at the Penmaenmawr Summer School); *The Four Seasons and the Archangels* (CW 229); *Harmony of the Creative Word* (CW 230); *The Supersensible Human* (CW 231), given in Holland for the founding of the Dutch society. On November 10, in response to the failed Hitler-Ludendorff putsch in Munich, Steiner closes his Berlin residence and moves the *Philosophisch-Anthroposophisch Verlag* (Press) to Dornach. On December 9, Steiner begins the serialization of his *Autobiography: The Course of My Life* (CW 28) in *Das Goetheanum.* It will continue to appear weekly, without a break, until his death. Late December–early January: Rudolf Steiner re-founds the Anthroposophical Society (about 12,000 members internationally) and takes over its leadership. The new board members are: Marie Steiner, Ita Wegman, Albert Steffen, Elisabeth Vreede, and Gunther Wachsmuth. (See *The Christmas Meeting for the Founding of the General Anthroposophical Society*, CW 260.) Accompanying lectures: *Mystery Knowledge and Mystery Centres* (CW 232); *World History in the Light of Anthroposophy* (CW 233). December 25: the Foundation Stone is laid (in the hearts of members) in the form of the 'Foundation Stone Meditation.'

1924: January 1: having founded the Anthroposophical Society and taken over its leadership, Rudolf Steiner has the task of 'reforming' it. The process begins with a weekly newssheet ('What's Happening in the Anthroposophical Society') in which Rudolf Steiner's 'Letters to Members' and 'Anthroposophical Leading Thoughts' appear (CW 26). The next step is the creation of a new esoteric class, the 'first class' of the 'University of Spiritual Science' (which was to have been followed, had Rudolf Steiner lived longer, by two more advanced classes). Then comes a new language for

Anthroposophy—practical, phenomenological, and direct; and Rudolf Steiner creates the model for the second Goetheanum. He begins the series of extensive 'karma' lectures (CW 235–40); and finally, responding to needs, he creates two new initiatives: biodynamic agriculture and curative education. After the middle of the year, rumours begin to circulate regarding Steiner's health. Lectures: January–February, *Anthroposophy* (CW 234); February: *Tone Eurythmy* (CW 278); June: *The Agriculture Course* (CW 327); June–July: *Speech Eurythmy* (CW 279); *Curative Education* (CW 317); August: (England, 'Second International Summer School'), *Initiation Consciousness: True and False Paths in Spiritual Investigation* (CW 243); September: *Pastoral Medicine* (CW 318). On September 26, for the first time, Rudolf Steiner cancels a lecture. On September 28, he gives his last lecture. On September 29, he withdraws to his studio in the carpenter's shop; now he is definitively ill. Cared for by Ita Wegman, he continues working, however, and writing the weekly installments of his *Autobiography* and *Letters to the Members/Leading Thoughts* (CW 26).

1925: Rudolf Steiner, while continuing to work, continues to weaken. He finishes *Extending Practical Medicine* (CW 27) with Ita Wegman. On March 30, around ten in the morning, Rudolf Steiner dies.

Index

M

N

O

P

R

S

T